£3·00

Discovering
the
Countryside
with
David
Bellamy
Woodland
Walks

Discovering the Countryside with
David Bellamy

Woodland Walks

Britain is fortunate in having a great variety of soils and climate and this diversity is reflected in our woodland types. These range from intensively managed broad-leaved woodlands in central and southern England to the ancient relict areas of pines in the Scottish Highlands. Each woodland habitat supports a particular society of animals and plants and in this book David Bellamy and his team of experts explore six different woods. There is a walk through a coppiced wood in spring; a search for badgers and butterflies in an elm wood in summer; a walk through an oak wood; a trek through a magnificent Caledonian pine forest; a journey out into the autumn in seach of fungi; and a tramp through a very wet wood (where else!) with Bellamy himself. The walks exemplify the interest that each type of wood can provide and these are prefaced by a 'fact spread' showing what common animals and plants to look out for, as well as areas with public access so the reader can discover the countryside for himself.

This is one of a series of books designed to help the reader understand the intricate world of our animals and plants. Each is based around an overall habitat and is illustrated with superb especially commissioned colour and black and white photographs.

Professor David Bellamy, who is consultant editor and contributor to this series of books, is one of the most popular botanists in Britain. He is a dedicated believer in the importance of communicating the excitement and enjoyment there is to be found in the study of natural history. Yet he is also very aware of the need for a new enlightened view on the conservation of our natural heritage, together with the important role that amateur naturalists can play in this. As an international authority on peat-lands and a television broadcaster he has travelled throughout the world but still maintains that Britain is his favourite country.

The Royal Society for Nature Conservation has collaborated in the production of this series of books. It is the national association for the 42 local Nature Conservation Trusts which form the major voluntary organisation concerned with all aspects of wildlife conservation in the United Kingdom. The Trusts have a combined membership of 140,000 and, together with the Society, own or manage over 1,300 nature reserves throughout the UK covering a variety of sites. Most Trusts have a full-time staff but the members themselves, with a wide range of skills, contribute greatly to all aspects of their work.

Places of interest

see Information pages
for further details

1 Beinn Eighe, Ross-shire
2 Glen Affric, Highlands
3 Glen More Forest Park, Highlands
4 Cairngorms, Highlands
5 Arriundle Wood, Highlands
6 Rannoch Forest, Tayside
7 Argyll Forest Park, Strathclyde
8 Queen Elizabeth Forest Park, Strathclyde
9 Loch Lomond, Strathclyde
10 Galloway Forest Park, Galloway
11 Glen Trool, Galloway
12 Border's/Kielder Forest Park, Borders/ Northumberland
13 Allen Banks, Northumberland
14 Borrowdale Woods, Cumbria

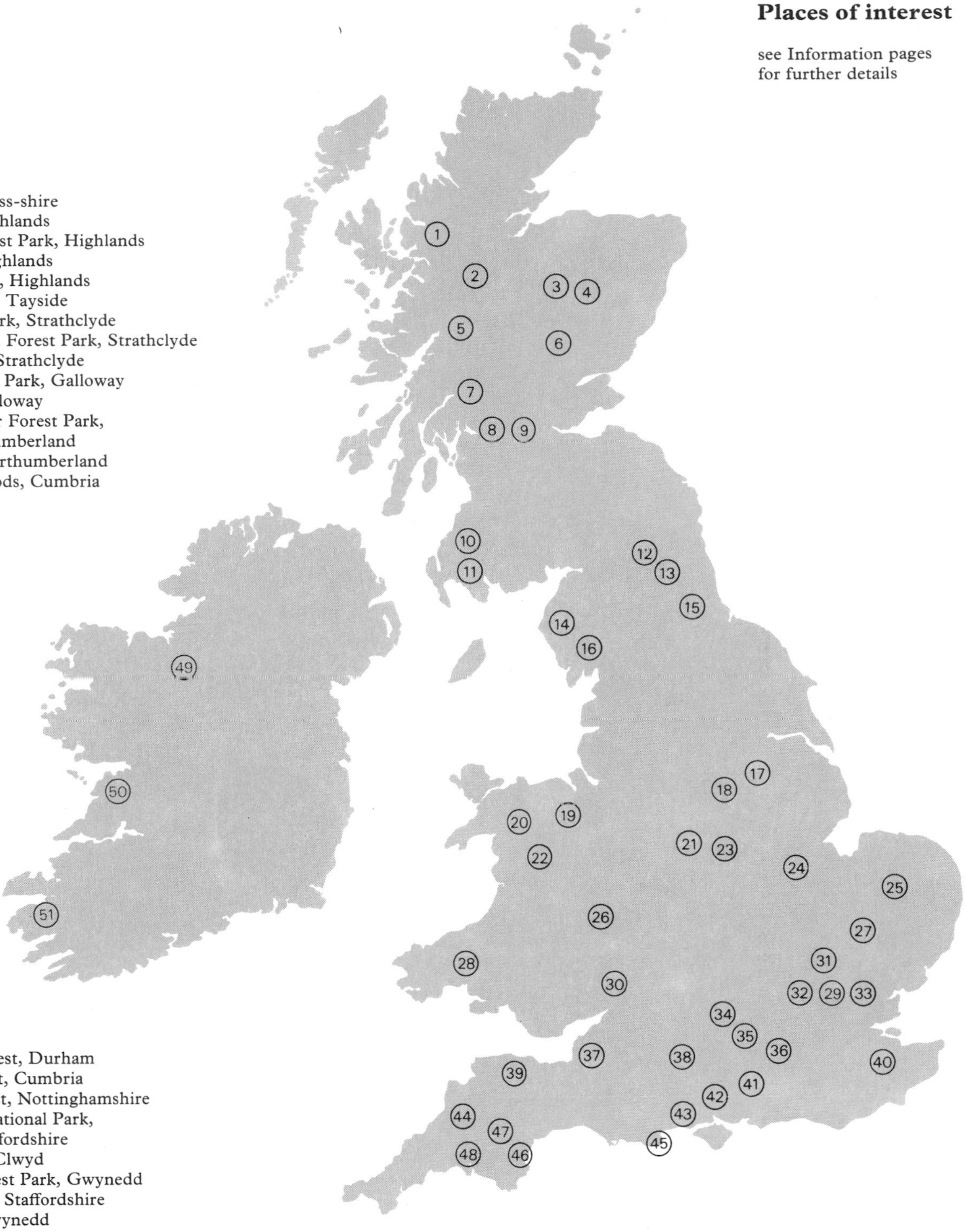

15 Hamsterley Forest, Durham
16 Grizedale Forest, Cumbria
17 Sherwood Forest, Nottinghamshire
18 Peak District National Park, Derbyshire/Staffordshire
19 Clwyd Forest, Clwyd
20 Snowdonia Forest Park, Gwynedd
21 Cannock Chase, Staffordshire
22 Maentwrog, Gwynedd
23 Charnwood Forest, Leicestershire
24 Woodwalton Fen, Cambridgeshire
25 Thetford Chase, Norfolk
26 Wyre Forest, Herefordshire/Worcestershire
27 Bradfield Woods, Suffolk
28 Dinas Woodlands, Dyfed
29 Hainault Forest, Essex
30 Forest of Dean, Herefordshire
31 Hatfield Forest, Essex
32 Epping Forest, Essex
33 Norsey Wood, Essex
34 Burnham Beeches, Buckinghamshire
35 Windsor Forest, Berkshire
36 Box Hill, Surrey
37 Ebbor Gorge, Somerset
38 Saversnake, Wiltshire
39 Lynmouth, Devon
40 Scords Wood, Kent
41 Selborne, Hampshire
42 Kingley Vale, Hampshire
43 New Forest, Hampshire/Dorset
44 Lydford Gorge, Devon
45 Brownsea Island, Dorset
46 Yarner Wood, Devon
47 Wistman's Wood, Devon
48 Goodameavy, Devon
49 Correl Glen Forest, Fermanagh
50 Burren, Clare
51 Killarney Oakwoods, Kerry

Discovering
the
Countryside
with
David
Bellamy

Hamlyn
London · New York · Sydney · Toronto

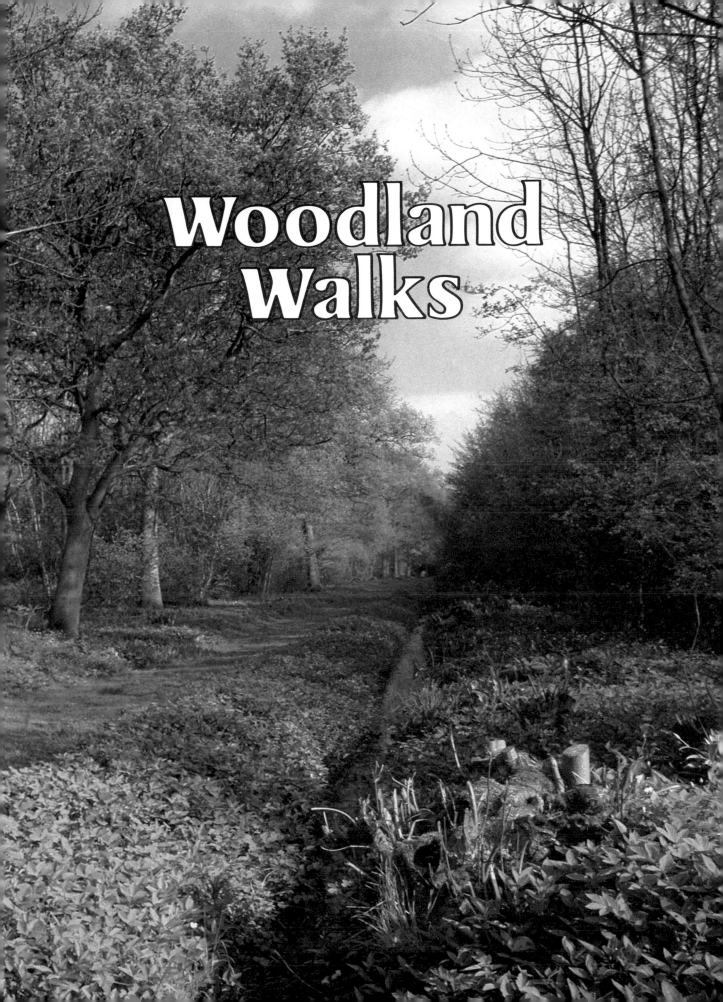

Woodland Walks

Acknowledgements

Artwork
Peter Crump 44, 81; Ian Garrard 88, 91, 95, 98 (from *The Hamlyn Guide to Trees of Britain and Europe*); Roger Gorringe 119 (from *The Hamlyn Guide to Edible and Medicinal Plants*); Richard Lewington 73; Laura Mason 108, 109; Mei-Lan Lim 14, 34, 55; The Tudor Art Agency Ltd. 59.

Photographs
Bruce Coleman – Owen Newman 75, Hans Reinhard 64; Wildlife Studies Ltd. 40, 67. All other photographs by Peter Loughran.

Published by
The Hamlyn Publishing Group Limited
London · New York · Sydney · Toronto
Astronaut House, Feltham, Middlesex, England

Printed in Great Britain

The Publisher and David Bellamy would like to thank the following organisations for their help in preparing this book.

Royal Society for Nature Conservation
Suffolk Trust for Nature Conservation
Bradfield Woods Management Committee
Scottish Wildlife Trust
Sussex Trust for Nature Conservation
Epping Forest Conservation Centre

In particular we would like to express our gratitude to the gallant team of experts: Peter Fordham, Alastair Sommerville, David and Simon Measures, David Streeter and Paul Moxey, whose hospitality, enthusiasm and vast knowledge of the countryside is only hinted at in these pages.

Country Code
Whenever and wherever you are out walking, please follow these simple rules:
- Guard against risk of fire
- Close all gates behind you, especially those at cattle grids, etc.
- Keep dogs under control
- Keep to paths across farmland – you have no right of way over surrounding land
- Avoid damaging fences, hedges and walls
- Leave no litter – take it away with you
- Safeguard water supplies
- Protect wildlife, plants and trees – do not pick flowers, leave them for others to enjoy
- Drive carefully on country roads
- Respect the life of the countryside – and you will be welcomed.

Foreword

The natural vegetation cover of the bulk of Britain is woodland. If you don't believe me, just stop cultivating your garden for the next fifty years or so and see what happens. Your choice blooms and well-kept lawn will soon disappear amongst a sea of scrub as nature re-asserts its hold on your real estate.

The exact make-up of this 'new forest' will be the only point in question. Will it be the same as that which covered the area before man dominated the land with his secateurs, mowing machines and all the other paraphernalia that allows the modern Joneses to keep up with the Capabilities of the Browns of the past?

When agricultural man first arrived in Britain, the scene was sylvan in the extreme: 95 per cent plus of these islands were covered with woodland. The lowlands of the north, the midlands and the south were dominated by oak, elm, Hazel and Alder, while in the highlands, especially in Scotland, the dominant trees were Scots Pine and birches.

The forest had already provided nomadic hunters with a surfeit of game: deer, boar, wild cattle, bison, wolf and even bears. In addition, they would have gathered edible roots, fruits and seeds to supplement their diets, and cut wood for their fires and the construction of their camps and habitations. However, these people had little or no effect on the forest itself – in fact, they lived much like the other forest inhabitants, as part of the balanced living system.

Neolithic man arrived on the scene around 5000 years ago, bringing with him knowledge of the husbandry of animals, the cultivation of crops and the technology of flint implements. Axes were used to cut down the trees, elm leaves were used as fodder, and pastures were created in the cleared areas where crops were also grown. When the soil nutrients were depleted the new farmers simply moved on, clearing new forest and leaving the old to regenerate as best it could. About 500 BC, the climate took a distinct change for the worse as wetter and colder conditions prevailed. It thus became more difficult for the warmth-demanding trees to grow, especially at high altitudes and latitudes. So man, with the help of the deteriorating climate, pushed the forest back, replacing it with other living communities. Some, like the blanket bogs of the uplands and the wetter west, were natural. Others, like the fields, villages and townships, were man-made and man-maintained. Yet others, best called semi-natural, were areas usually unwanted by man at that particular time, and were left to nature's own healing devices.

The dual economies of farmer and hunter up to the Middle Ages and beyond, kept the woodlands as an important part of any landscape, at least for the landed gentry. Coppicing and pollarding, which probably developed by accident during the period of flint-axe technology, became methods for the maintained productivity of managed forests. Those forest that remained were still a focal point for an ever expanding population and were of importance to an Iron Age people right up to the Industrial Revolution when coal and the harnessed power of steam pushed the human population of Britain towards ever increasing limits.

Our native woodlands, whether natural or coppiced, fell into disuse as man's endeavours turned in other directions. Frequently, they were replaced by plantations often of a single and usually exotic species introduced from other lands, each monoculture managing to produce good straight timber as fast and as economically as possible.

It was this de-forested landscape that the conservation movement inherited earlier this century, disjunct scraps of woodland, at best linked by old hedgerows. Already many of the most important sites are in the care of the nation, either through the auspices of the Nature Conservancy Council or the National Trust. The County Conservation Trusts, under the umbrella of the Royal Society for Nature Conservation, are tending and restoring other woodland sites by lease or purchase. Modern economic forestry, led by the Forestry Commission, already considers amenity and wildlife concerns as an important part of the productive whole and Britain's plantations look to a brighter and more diverse future.

This book concerns this modern scene, introducing the reader to the experience that comes with a full understanding of woodland. Each of the chapters, which is prefaced by two pages of background information, is centred around a walk which takes the reader out into different types of woodland, from the ancient Caledonian pine forests to the oakwoods of the Sussex Weald. Our experts lend their own personal touch to each outing, bringing their wealth of experience and enthusiasm to the walks.

Discovering
the
Countryside
with
David
Bellamy

Woodland
Walks

Bellamy's Valley
Woodland.

Contents

A Coppiced Wood
in Spring
with Peter Fordham

Photography
by Peter Loughran

Bellamy's Valley Woodland

You don't have to go to a National Nature Reserve to enjoy the woodland scene and everything it offers for the natural historian. To prove it, I chose a scrap of woodland, used and abused by man, set on the edge of one of the great industrial conurbations of the North East. I had visited it on many occasions before, and I will go back again and again, because the more you know, the more you find of interest. I will never fully come to terms with the fact that the growth of a few trees can so change a habitat and that a copse, however small, has a life-style all of its own. Neither will I ever understand all the intricacies of the inter-relationships between soil, plants and animals that make a wood what it is : a lifetime's work for any naturalist.

Our valley woodland with its fringe canopy of birches and Rowans and its rich ground vegetation.

Information

The smaller and steeper valleys and the marshlands of Britain contain some of our most interesting woodlands. This because the terrain they cover has proved either too steep, too wet, or just too small for the farmer to fully exploit. However, some of them have nevertheless been cut for timber or coppiced for firewood, and in upland areas they are frequently open to heavy grazing by sheep. Despite this, they represent some of the most 'natural' woodland in Britain and can often show a surprising diversity within a small area.

The increasing moisture content in the soil as you approach the valley bottom and the effect of mineral deposition at the lower levels mean that it is possible to detect a degree of zonation in the woodland vegetation. In our example of a 'valley woodland' the catchment area is largely acidic, giving a zonation that starts with a fringe of birch and Rowan, moving through a mixed canopy of oak and Ash, to Alders and willows in the valley bottom. On some of the more lime-rich soils, the upper zones (in southern England) may be dominated by Beech as, for example, on the famous Beech hangers at Selborne in Hampshire. In north and west Britain, Ash tends to be the main tree species, with elms, Sessile Oak and, in some areas, whitebeams also contributing to the canopy.

In the valley bottoms, the ground vegetation can be very diverse with many 'fen' species such as Greater Tussock Sedge growing on the rich peaty soils. Further up the slope, typical woodland plants such as Bluebells and Honeysuckle (on acid soils), and Dog's Mercury and Sanicle (on more base soils) can be found. The dense shade and the rather toxic leaf-litter produced by the Beech mean that its ground flora can be comparatively sparse. However, lower down on all types of soil the humid environment is ideal for the growth of ferns and other non-flowering plants such as lichens, liverworts and mosses.

Some plants to look out for:

Trees
Silver Birch *Betula pendula*
Downy Birch *Betula pubescens*
Rowan *Sorbus aucuparia*
Ash *Fraxinus excelsior*
Beech *Fagus sylvatica*
Sessile Oak *Quercus petraea*
Pedunculate Oak *Quercus robur*
Holly *Ilex aquifolium*
Alder *Alnus glutinosa*
Willows and sallows *Salix*
Guelder Rose *Viburnum opulus*
Hawthorn *Crataegus monogyna*
Buckthorn *Rhamnus catharticus*
Elder *Sambucus nigra*

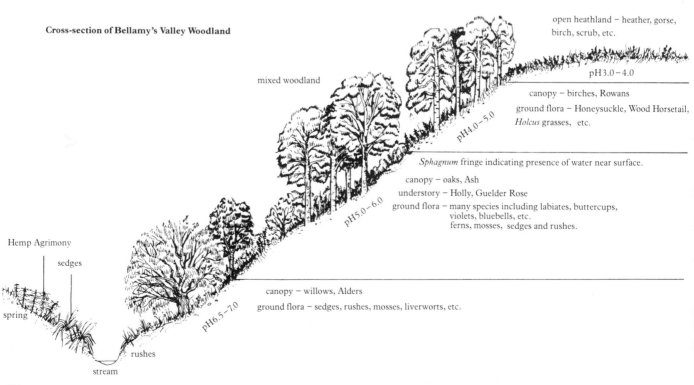

Cross-section of Bellamy's Valley Woodland

open heathland – heather, gorse, birch, scrub, etc.

pH3.0–4.0

canopy – birches, Rowans
ground flora – Honeysuckle, Wood Horsetail, *Holcus* grasses, etc.

mixed woodland

pH4.0–5.0

Sphagnum fringe indicating presence of water near surface.

canopy – oaks, Ash
understory – Holly, Guelder Rose
ground flora – many species including labiates, buttercups, violets, bluebells, etc. ferns, mosses, sedges and rushes.

pH5.0–6.0

Hemp Agrimony

sedges

canopy – willows, Alders
ground flora – sedges, rushes, mosses, liverworts, etc.

pH6.5–7.0

spring

rushes

stream

Ferns and their allies

Wood Horsetail *Equisetum sylvaticum*
Great Horsetail *Equisetum telmateia*
Male Fern *Dryopteris filix-mas*
Borrer's Male Fern *Dryopteris pseudomas*

Broad Buckler Fern *Dryopteris dilatata*
Lady Fern *Athyrium filix-femina*
Hard Fern *Blechnum spicant*
Bracken *Pteridium aquilinum*

Flowering Plants

	Acid to Neutral soils	Neutral		Basic soils
wetter	Rosebay Willowherb (*Epilobium angustifolium*) Bramble (*Rubus fruticosus*) Barren Strawberry (*Potentilla sterilis*) Bluebell (*Endymion nonscriptus*) Honeysuckle (*Lonicera periclymenum*)	Tufted Hair Grass (*Deschampsia caespitosa*) Great Hairy Woodrush (*Luzula sylvatica*) Wood Anemone (*Anemone nemorosa*) Bugle (*Ajuga reptans*) Nettle (*Urtica dioica*) Common Dog Violet (*Viola riviniana*)	Soft Rush (*Juncus effusus*) Remote Sedge (*Carex remota*) Ragged Robin (*Lychnis flos-cuculi*) Primrose (*Primula vulgaris*) Early Purple Orchid (*Orchis mascula*) Creeping Soft Grass (*Holcus mollis*)	Hemp Agrimony (*Eupatorium cannabinum*) Hemlock Water-dropwort (*Oenanthe crocata*) Water Avens (*Geum rivale*) Sanicle (*Sanicula europaea*) Dog's Mercury (*Mercurialis perennis*) Herb Robert (*Geranium robertianum*)
drier	Common Cow-wheat (*Melampyrum pratense*) Wood Sorrel (*Oxalis acetosella*) Wood Meadow-grass (*Poa nemoralis*)	Creeping Buttercup (*Ranunculus repens*) Hedge Woundwort (*Stachys sylvatica*) Marsh Thistle (*Cirsium palustre*)	Wood Melick Grass (*Melica uniflora*) Common Hairy Woodrush (*Luzula pilosa*)	Herb Bennet (*Geum urbanum*) Giant Fescue Grass (*Festuca gigantea*) Enchanter's Nightshade (*Circaea lutetiana*)

Sites

The following is a small selection of some interesting valley woodlands from throughout Britain. They cover a wide range of types from upland woods, which have survived on steep cliffy banks, to beautiful woodlands which cover the sides of lowland rivers. It is suggested that you consult some of the many regional guides before intending to visit any of the sites.

Arriundle Wood, Highlands. National Nature Reserve. An interesting area of valley woodland beside the Strontian River. Good tree species: Sessile Oak, birch, Rowan; many mosses and lichens. Nature Trail.

Allen Banks, Northumberland. National Trust. Mature deciduous valley woodland. Pleasant walks along the river-side.

Peak District National Park, Derbyshire/Staffordshire. Excellent examples of valley woodlands on Carboniferous Limestone. Ash is the predominant species with a rich ground flora.

Woodwalton Fen, Cambridgeshire. National Nature Reserve. Important reserve amongst area of intensive agriculture, showing wide variety of fen species including Alder carr.

Wicken Fen, Cambridgeshire. National Trust. Fenland reserve with well-developed Alder carr.

Dinas Woodlands, Dyfed. Interesting area of valley woodlands. Sessile Oak is the predominant tree. Many lichens and bryophytes as well as good bird life.

Forest of Dean, Wye Valley, Herefordshire. Large area of mixed wood including many unusual broad-leaved species. Forestry Commission Nature Reserves at Symonds Yat and Wyndcliff. Interesting bird life including Pied Flycatcher.

Ebbor Gorge, Somerset. National Nature Reserve. Exceptional valley woodland on Carboniferous Limestone. Predominately Ash but with some whitebeams as well. Good ground flora. Nature trail.

Lynmouth, Devon. National Trust. Beautiful valley woodland 'discovered' by Shelley, with varied selection of broad-leaved trees including oaks and whitebeams.

Lydford Gorge, Devon. National Trust. Valley woodland with good selection of broad-leaved trees, lichens and mosses. Interesting ground flora. Popular spot with waterfall.

Wistman's Wood, Devon. Forest Nature Reserve on the edge of Dartmoor. Relict Pedunculate Oak woodland with very good lichens and mosses.

Yarner Wood, Devon. National Nature Reserve. Large area of mixed woodland with Pedunculate and Sessile Oaks, Ash and Alders. Good lichens and mosses. Nature Trail.

Goodameavy, Devon. National Trust. Area of oakwood beside River Plym. Good lichens and mosses. Rich in industrial archaeological remains.

Selborne, Hampshire. National Trust. Famous Beech Hangers overlooking village immortalised by Gilbert White.

Scords Wood, Kent. National Trust. Area of mixed woodland including Alder carr. Good ground flora.

Wherever you are in Britain, yes, even if you are in the largest city of all, you are within the catchment of a river. All rivers are fed by streams and they are, in turn, fed by smaller and smaller streams and eventually by springs, run-off and seepage. Now, I find these tiny steams the most exciting places to visit in any landscape. They are wonderfully squishy spots where you just can't help getting your feet wet and, what is more, they are usually either too steep or too wet for agricultural use and so have been left to their own devices. In other words, they are tiny oases of semi-naturalness in an otherwise man-managed landscape.

Today I have come out to such a place, a very ordinary bit of Britain not all that far from the sprawling conurbation of Tees and Wearside, in fact, if I stand on tiptoe I can just see the roofs of Chester-le-Street. It is a tiny scrap of woodland flanked by heathland, which is in a pretty bad state of management: scarred by spoil heaps, overridden by motor bikes and over-burned by fires, which are lit with monotonous regularity when the weather is warm and dry. But as you walk downslope, into the valley bottom, the picture changes, for below the seepage line the soil is so wet that it is protected from the run of the fire and so woodland can hold its own special sway.

My feet are now decidedly damp, for this is the point at which the rain water which has collected from the catchment area behind me emerges at the surface. The rain which fell back up there has percolated down through the heathland soils and dissolved some along the way and thus become enriched by certain minerals, some of which are essential for the growth of the woodland plants. Here on the margin of the wood the seepage lines will not flow during the driest part of the year but lower down the flow will be more permanent until finally at the bottom the soils will be saturated throughout the year along beside the central stream. These wettest soils are likely to be richest in minerals and hence those close beside the stream have the greatest diversity of plant life.

I hasten to point out that it doesn't matter if you don't have heathland in your local valley, the same principles work even if the valley bottom is set in well-run arable land. That is, of course, so long as the farmer hasn't put in land drains and tarted up the central stream. Please remember the golden rules: farmers do a fantastically important job in our countryside, so always ask permission before going on farmland and when you are there always follow the country code.

Now we are ready to explore the magic of what I like to call 'Bottom Woodland'.

It's a lovely sunny day and we have just passed from the full brunt of the sunlight into the dappled shade of the woodland edge and the first trees we come to are birches. Everyone knows a birch tree, don't they? Silvery white bark and a characteristic

Dry heath blasted in more ways than one – overridden by motor-bikes, overburned and scarred by spoil heaps. But in the valley bottom there is an oasis of woodland.

shape. Easy isn't it? Well, be careful because there are two types: the Downy Birch (*Betula pubescens*) and the Silver Birch (*Betula pendula*). This one has nice knobbly bark at the base, figured to produce rectangular bosses, which is a characteristic of Silver Birch. Then a little lower down the slope is a Downy Birch, which has a smooth bark almost to the base of the tree. These two types of tree are producing welcome shade and an immediate drop in temperature and light intensity. A new environment in which shade loving plants will dominate, and there's one of them, *Equisetum sylvaticum*, the Wood Horsetail. A rarity down south, it was the first woodland plant to greet me in abundance when I moved up into the North East. What is more, it is the easiest of all our horsetails to identify for it is the only one whose branches are branched, producing the effect of a delicate feathery plant. However, handling it will immediately show its rough nature, for like all the scouring rushes (which is the other common name for the horsetails) its tissues are packed with silica. Before the days of 'Brillo' pads and wire wool, the busy housewife would nip out into the garden, grab a bunch of *Equisetum* and polish the saucepans. You can try it for yourself with the Common Horsetail – an all too often troublesome weed of the garden. A word of warning, never use it anywhere near your super non-stick kitchen pans, the scouring rushes are much too tough for Teflon.

The scouring rushes are members of the Calamophyta, the great group of plants which included the Giant Horsetails of the past, the remains of which helped to form the coal upon which the affluence of the North East was founded. What is more, the tiny stream which has formed the valley is cutting its way down towards the coal measures in which the fossils of those long extinct plants may be found. So this delicate looking woodland plant provides a very real link towards the past, a past in which the dinosaurs reigned supreme. I like to lay down and get the horsetails in close focus and try to imagine a *Tyranosaurus* plodging its way through the undergrowth.

We are still only a few metres from the open heathland and yet everything says that I am in a woodland habitat. The canopy is a mixture of birch and Rowan. Rowan, Mountain Ash or, to give it its proper name, *Sorbus aucuparia*, is a tree which, with its general shape, compound leaves and scarlet

fruits, is easy to identify at any time of the year. It is a tree which everyone should know, and there down on the ground is another well-known plant with a really terrible Latin name, *Lonicera periclymenum*. No, I can't say it either, but I do like the scent of its flowers. It is Honeysuckle. Here it is forming an untidy mass on the ground, but over there it is in its more typical form, dangling liana-like from a tree. See how it twists in a clockwise fashion, so tight that it has constricted and deformed the branch which is providing its support.

The dominant grass hereabouts is the Wavy Hair Grass, *Deschampsia flexuosa*. Now, I know that many people say, 'Oh grasses, they're much too difficult to identify,' and they leave them alone. This really is a pity because not only are they very beautiful but they are very abundant in most habitats. Take a look at this one. From a distance a wonderful dark green mat, cool,

We are just inside the wood under mature birch and already the ground flora has become more diverse. Here are the delicate fronds of Wood Horsetail (*Equisetum sylvaticum*) together with Bracken and Honeysuckle.

Above **Honeysuckle** (*Lonicera periclymenum*) **forming an untidy mat on the ground. A woodland climber looking for support.**

Above right **The flowerhead** (**panicle**) of *Deschampsia flexuosa.* **Who said grasses aren't beautiful?**

soft and damp to the touch. Look closer and you can see that each leaf is like a hair or bristle, or, to use the proper botanical term, setaceous. And there it is beginning to flower and is showing one of its most distinctive characteristics. There below the developing flower head, a short leaf sticks out but follow it down and you will see that the main part of the leaf is a sheath which encloses the flower stalk all the way down to the base.

Setaceous leaves are usually characteristic of plants which live under the threat of water stress; the reduction of the leaf blade helps to cut down water loss. Well, here on the edge of the woodland, a dry summer can create real problems especially for the plants which root in the surface layers of the soil. In effect, the trees and other deeper rooting plants will 'pinch' all the water, leaving the surface layers dry, hence the xeromorphic (water saving) characteristic of some of the plants.

Down slope just a few more metres and once again the character of the woodland floor has changed dramatically. The thing which really 'cools the cockles of my feet' is that it is now much wetter. We are entering what I like to call real 'plodging country' and we should be able to find my favourite plants. Yes, there they are, the bog mosses or Sphagna. Excuse me for a moment, while I sing their praises. Well, I should do for I have spent the last twenty-seven years of my life, part immersed in the study of their habitat.

Most of the Sphagna are found out on the open fells and in really squishy places, like bogs and fens, and when we come to deal with those in another book I will let you into their real secrets. There are, however, some which do inhabit wet woodlands and here we have our first, *Sphagnum squarrosum.* Botanically, 'squarrose' means that the leaves stick out all around the stem in an almost star-like fashion, and there they are. This one is a big robust 'chunky knit' *Sphagnum*, unlike the very dark green one over there, which is much more delicate and is called *Sphagnum fimbriatum.* Please be careful where you put your feet; in a place like this you can destroy the habitat in seconds. All you need to do is take up a single stem of Sphagnum and with the aid of a lens all will be revealed.

See how delicate they are; neither can stand up on their own. No, not even the squarrose one. All the bog mosses have very weak and brittle stems. They cannot stand up by themselves and so they grow in great swelling masses, each separate plant, as it were, leaning on its next door neighbour.

I must admit that the bog mosses are not the easiest plants to identify, at least down to specific level, so I think that at this stage it is best first to say that it is a *Sphagnum* and just marvel at the way in which the large swelling hummocks and mats pick out the wettest spots here along the first true seepage line, while the more permanent ground water is still quite acid.

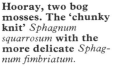

Hooray, two bog mosses. The 'chunky knit' *Sphagnum squarrosum* with the more delicate *Sphagnum fimbriatum.*

Perhaps at this point, a word about acidity would be appropriate. The contents of your car battery are very acid and very corrosive. Acidity in the ecological sense lacks this corrosive power and is a balance between the acid and the alkaline, or basic, substances present in the soil. This balance is measured on what is called a scale of pH. The scale rises from 1, which is very acid, to 14, which is very alkaline, with 7 in the middle when the acids and bases are in balance or neutrality. Rain, though in essence pure water, is slightly acidic and thus gradually leaches the bases from any soil. If these are not replaced then the soil becomes more and more acid, as on the heath where a pH of 3.2, and even lower, is possible on a summer's day. Here, on the permanent seepage line, the soils are fortunately enriched by the bases leached from above and the pH is 4.2 and, as if to prove it, other less acid-tolerant plants are present just below the fringe of Sphagna.

The Soft Rush, *Juncus effusus*, is a common plant of mineral soils on moorland and in pastures where the farmer hasn't quite got the drainage right. Feel how smooth it is, no ridges, a completely cylindrical stem, soft to the touch, so soft that you can squash it flat. Take a look inside (it's a common plant so one leaf won't hurt), you can see it is full of an 'airy-fairy' tissue – a white pith, which, in actual fact, consists of a mass of large holes held together by a meshwork of living cells. This very squashy tissue is called aerenchyma and is found in all truly aquatic plants. All the rushes like growing with their 'feet' wet and they are, again, a group which many people leave alone, on the assumption that they are too difficult to identify. All I can say is have a go and you will find that they are quite easy. Here is a tufted plant with a smooth soft stem, *Juncus effusus*, growing here in its natural habitat – the wet bits in a woodland. Before the advent of man into the wooded landscapes of Britain, this was probably its main habitat. But as the forests were cleared the wetter spots in the farmers' fields became colonised by the plant, which has now turned out to be a very aggressive weed species and not easy to eradicate.

This plant is thus another link with the past, with a time, a mere 5000 years ago, when much of Britain was under natural woodland, some of which must have looked much like this. The presence of *Sphagnum fimbriatum* takes us back even further, for it was one of the first plants to grow when the great ice sheets of the last glaciation melted hereabouts, some 17000 years ago.

Sorry, I am getting carried away! We've looked at a grass, a rush, and now there's a sedge. This is another group of plants which all but the experts seem to shun. This is the Remote-flowered Sedge, *Carex remota*. Beautiful isn't it, with its remotely set flower heads, each nestling in the axil of a long leaf-like bract. Take the top of the stem in your fingers and gently roll it, plonk –

The inside story of a **Soft Rush** (*Juncus effusus*). **The delicate pith is a meshwork of living tissue called aerenchyma.**

plonk – plonk! It doesn't roll, as it is three sided, the trade mark of the sedge family. In fact, if you take a close look you will find that everything about the plant happens in threes. The leaves come off in threes; the parts of the flower are in threes. There it is, not a grass, not a rush, but a sedge – the third of the great groups of Graminoids, grass-like plants.

Three metres further on into the wood, perhaps half a metre deeper down the slope of the valley, and we are now in real mixed woodland with a dense canopy, the like of which must have covered an enormous part of lowland Britain in the past; a scrap of history. The canopy above consists of birch, oak and Ash with a little Alder, each tree occupying its own chosen spot in the un-even terrain of the valley side. There are bumps and depressions around and through

Above **The Remote-flowered Sedge** (*Carex remota*) **each flower-head sits in the axil of a long leafy bract.**

which the spring and seepage waters make their way down towards the central stream. Below the main canopy, there are saplings of the dominant trees, and there is a Holly, *Ilex aquifolium*, the only British representative of the plant family, the Aquifoliaceae. The grass family is the Gramineae, the rush family the Juncaceae, the sedge family the Cyperaceae – now we are really getting our-selves plugged into botany and I am sinking in a particularly wet bit of woodland. Other members of the shrub layer are the beauti-ful Guelder Rose, *Vibernum opulus*. Now that tells me that the conditions hereabouts are less acid than higher up on the valley sides.

Excuse me while I get my feet unstuck from the mud! I don't think I would have liked to have been an Ancient Briton travel-ling through a landscape covered in wood-

land like this. It can't have been easy, not because of the dense undergrowth, but because of the land drainage. Those dense impenetrable stands of Bramble and Sting-ing Nettles, which we find in our man-managed countrysides, are not natural. In fact, the undergrowth of mixed woodland is usually very open in character, for a wood-land is a living community in which there is space for a whole variety of plants. Here, where the soil is around pH 5·5 the variety is much greater, in fact, everywhere I look there is a different plant. I will refrain from giving you a long list and will just mention some of the commonest of the plants.

This is Hedge or Wood Woundwort, *Stachys sylvatica*, and there, close beside it, Bugle, another member of the same family. See how similar the flowers are both in shape and arrangement on the stem. Both

thrive best in the shade, producing a welcome splash of colour on the sombre woodland floor. Of all the woodland plants, I think that the woundwort has the most revolting smell. No, not the flower, but the leaf – crush one and you will see. As you squeeze it, feel its soft woolly texture. It is in fact covered with hairs, and therein lies both its virtue and name. If you do happen to cut yourself while in the field a leaf from this plant applied to the wound will soon stop the bleeding. The active principle is in all probability the hairs, which help the blood to clot. The chemical, which produces the nasty smell, may also have some astringent property. Who knows? But it works. What a nasty smell! The fantastic thing is that many of the ingredients which go into the best perfumes smell pretty terrible in their pure form. It is the mixture of many pro-

The spiny leaves of **Holly** (*Ilex aquifolium*). This tree is a common element in the under-story of our woods.

ducts originally derived from plants and animals which produce the famous names in the perfume world.

Beyond the stand of *Stachys* is a small bank covered with ferns, and even from here I can see there are three, no, four different species. So let's get plugged into the ferns. Each has an underground stem or rhizome from which spring the great tufts of leaves. Yes, each one of those is a compound leaf, the central bit is not a stem, but a leaf stalk or petiole. Start counting the divisions of the leaf of this one. The petiole bears pinnae (division one) the pinnae bear pinnules (division two) and the pinnules themselves are lobed (division three). So here we have a three pinnate leaf and look at the petiole itself – the base is covered with large papery scales, each one of which has a dark centre. All in all, that tells me it is the Broad Buckler Fern, *Dryopteris austriaca*.

Next door to it is a much lighter coloured fern, the fronds of which are only twice pinnate, and the scales are a uniform light brown, making this the Male Fern, *Dryopteris filix-mas*. There in the background is what, at first sight, appears to be the same species, but look at the petiole almost obscured by a dense covering of ginger-brown scales, and also at the base of each pinnae is a dark patch; this is Borrer's Male Fern, *Dryopteris pseudomas*, named after a famous botanist. Wouldn't it be nice to have such a super plant named after you?

A bit further on at the base of the bank there is an altogether more delicate fern which is aptly named *Athyrium filix-femina*, the Lady Fern. Isn't she beautiful? Her leaves are again two pinnate but if you turn them over you will see the characteristic that tells me that this is a different fern genus. There down either side of each pinnule are some elongate almost crescent-shaped scales. Compare the shape with those on the other three ferns, and you will see that in all the other three, the scales are shaped like a tiny kidney. These scales are called indusia, and whatever shape they are, they cover and protect groups of sporangia, which are the reproduction organs of the fern.

Ferns do not bear flowers, they bear spores. When ripe, the spores are released and being very light they are blown about on the wind. Those which land in the right place (and for these four ferns that would be a damp woodland floor) germinate and grow, though not to form a new pinnate fern plant as we know it, but to form a small green scale about the size of my little finger nail. The small scale or prothallus, as it is called, bears the organs of sexual reproduction. The female organs produce eggs and the male, sperm. The sperm, when released, swim through the surface film of water down on the damp woodland floor to fertilize the eggs. This is one reason why ferns are more abundant in damp places. The result is a new baby fern plant which in time will grow up to be just like its original parent.

I can't find any prothalli but there is a baby Broad Buckler no more than two centimetres tall, and there at the bottom is the shrivelled scale, which is the other half of its complex life cycle.

I like to come here in the winter when many of the giant fern leaves have died back and you can see the top of the underground stems protected by a mass of scales and bearing a crown of next year's leaves, each one rolled up like a bishop's crozier. The most beautiful of all in its winter glory is *Dryopteris pseudomas* – its mass of ginger scales, glowing in the winter sun, gives away its presence and acts as a homing beacon for the dancing displays of the winter gnats. I have stood here in winter, right on this spot, and watched the Roe Deer grazing and the gnats enjoying the warmth of the sun's rays slanting down through the leafless canopy. Today, there are no Roe Deer in sight, my noisy commentary has frightened them all away; thank goodness the plants can't move! What a variety there is here, please excuse

The delicate fronds of **Lady Fern** (*Athyrium filix-femina*); **one of our more common woodland ferns.**

Below **Scaly or Borrer's Male Fern** (*Dryopteris pseudomas*) **in the shade of the wood. These magnificent ferns have a mass of gingery-coloured papery scales at the base of their petioles. Do not confuse them with the Broad Buckler Fern whose scales have a dark centre.**

the list: Wild Angelica, no, not the one that you put in the cakes at Christmas but a close relative; Wood Club Rush, *Scirpus sylvaticus*, another grass-like plant from another family, the Juncaginaceae, the members of which instantly identify themselves by the long white hairs at the base of the leaves; *Valeriana officinalis*, an official plant, which means that it was used in medicine and mentioned in the *Pharmacopeia* for 'Tincture of Valerian'; it was used for heart complaints. What else can we find? Marsh Thistle, instantly identifiable by its rosette of prickly leaves and the habitat – damp areas in woodland; and there's Water Avens and Water Mint, goodness, I should have been able to smell that. When tormented by gnats and midges in a place like this I always like to rub a mint leaf on my face – I don't know whether it helps to keep the insects away but it sure makes me feel better. Amongst the mint are the undoubted leaves of Water Violet, *Viola palustris*, and then below them

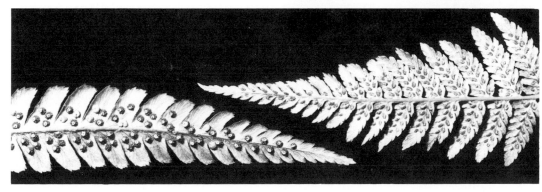

The underside of the tip of the pinnae of **Lady Fern** (above) and **Borrer's Male Fern** (below). **The sori can be clearly seen. Those on the Lady Fern are crescent to oblong shaped whereas the ones on the Borrer's Male Fern are large and kidney-shaped.**

The damp ground near the valley bottom can have an immense variety of plants growing on it. Here beneath some Alder trees are the yellow flowers of Marsh Hawksbeard (*Crepis paludosa***) amidst a panoply of horsetails, ferns, rushes and sedges.**

all are the mosses and liverworts hiding and almost hidden, down close to the damp soil.

I have said it once and I will say it again and again, a woodland is a community of plants, a community in which there are many jobs to be done and in which it is always a case of a job well done. The trees form the canopy of a multi-decked 'solar cell': trees, shrubs, ferns, herbs, mosses and liverworts, the members of each layer adapted to live and thrive in the environment which is produced in part by the presence of the others round about. The trees must be sun loving, whereas the mosses and liverworts must be shade tolerant.

Here amongst the mixture of mosses and liverworts is another feature of this community and a very important one in shaping the characteristics of the environment. It looks just like a 'clove pomander', you know those round things covered with cloves that you can buy at avant-guard 'ooh-aah shops'. Its presence tells me that I am now down into the next and final forest zone and a quick glance upwards confirms the fact that the dominant trees are now Alder (*Alnus glutinosa*).

The 'clove pomanders' are, in fact, masses of nodules which are produced on the roots of the Alder. Living inside the nodules are

return for this cheap supply of fertilizer the Alder provides a protected home for the bacteria. We thus have a case of symbiosis or mutual help, a union from which both participants derive benefit.

The best place in which to see these unusual root nodules is in the actual stream, for there the soil is being constantly washed away, exposing the root system of the trees. Yes, I was right – there are great masses of them, washed clear ready for inspection. I am, however, not going to paddle in the stream because I am afraid it is polluted. Not far up stream is a farm, with a number of animal houses. The effluent from these goes through a septic tank and then discharges into the stream. When the septic tank is working properly the organic matter is broken down and the partly purified water, rich in phosphates and nitrates, flows into the stream. When it isn't working that

colonies of many millions of simple organisms, bacteria, to be exact. Many bacteria cause disease harming the plant or animal in which they live. These particular bacteria cause great deformity of the roots of the host plant and at first sight it might look like a nasty disease. This is, however, not the case as the bacteria living inside the roots cause no harm at all. They in fact do exactly the reverse; they help the Alder tree to live and grow more efficiently. These bacteria are able to fix nitrogen from the atmosphere and turn it into nitrate 'fertilizer', some of which is used by the Alder and other plants growing round about. In

well or is overloaded then I am afraid that some of the organic matter gets into the stream causing all sorts of problems. Looking along the stream bank I can see the effects of both types of pollution.

Those grey flocculent masses floating in the backwater are sewage bacteria, nature's own way of breaking down the excess organic matter being poured into the stream. Given a chance they will help complete the job started in the septic tank. The other form of pollution, enrichment with fertilizing minerals, is shown by the bright green nature of the banks of the stream. Here everything is growing well, thanks to a

Here is one of my 'clove-pomanders' on the roots of an Alder. This gall-like formation contains millions of bacteria which are helping the tree to fix nitrogen in the soil.

The valley bottom with a little stream winding its way at the centre of the wood. Along its edges are stands of Stinging Nettles (*Urtica dioica*).

continuous supply of nitrate and phosphate and, as if to prove it, there are great masses of Stinging Nettles, *Urtica dioica*, and the one with smaller leaves and an even worse sting, *Urtica urens*. I always say it's called *Urtica* cos it 'urts! Both thrive in areas rich in phosphate – one reason why they are so common in waste places and rubbish dumps. Amongst the bright green of the nettle beds are some of the more natural denizens of the river bank, again all thriving on enrichment, for even without the chicken farm the stream brings down, in its natural course, much eroded material rich in minerals. There is *Chrysosplenium oppositifolium*, the Opposite-leaved Golden Saxifrage, its English name is almost as much of a mouthful. The dominant grass here is *Holcus mollis*, very easy to identify with its prominent nodes, which look not unlike hairy knees. A grass consists of a stem which is divided into nodes, which are often swollen, and from which the leaves arise, and long thinner internodes which are usually sheathed by the leaf base. A close relative, *Holcus lanatus*, is growing nearby and its nodes are not nearly as prominent. What is more, it is hairy all over, including its nodes and internodes. On a cool autumn morning when the mist rises from the ground it often appears to be trapped as a layer, just above the ground by this hairy grass, hence perhaps its common name, Yorkshire Fog.

In amongst the two *Holci*, is another much more robust grass growing in rank tussocks.

If you are very careful and press your hand down into the tussock you will feel that the leaves are covered in sharp spines. They are made of pure silca and are very sharp, so sharp that if you are not careful you will have to go back and seek the astringent help of the woundwort. The name of this sharp grass is *Deschampsia caespitosa*, the Tufted Hair Grass. Yes, big as it is, it is closely related to the deep dark green one we saw higher up in the woodland. A comparison of their flower structures will show you why.

I am now going to try to cross the stream without getting too polluted, a big jump should do it. . . . Aaah, straight into a Stining Nettle and back into the water! Oh well, now I am here, I can take a closer look at the stream bank and the bed.

Here the bed is covered with a thick green mat of algae. Many algae are slimy to the touch but this one is quite rough, and stringy. It's *Cladophora*, another indicator of polluted water. I'd better get out. However, before I do there are two things of great interest. Down close beside the water is a large spreading tuft of one of our largest thallose liverworts, *Marchantia polymorpha*. Thallose means undivided into stems and leaves, the plant body, as you can see, is a flat thallus which is branched so that it looks not unlike the lobes of a liver, hence their name. Remember 'wort' is the old English term for plant and, indeed, in the olden days they were used to help cure jaundice and other complaints of the liver. Mind you, if

branched and does not stand upright but lies flat on the ground. Its name is *Bracythecium rutabulum*; a moss which doesn't mind a little bit of eutrophication.

Over the past twenty-two years, I must have brought many thousands of students through this wood and I always stop to sing the praises of the mosses and liverworts. One reason why I like them so much is that winter or summer, they are always there, a source of great interest, waiting to be identified. What is more, all you need for adequate study is a couple of stems, no more, and these can give you hours of pleasure during the long winter evenings, for with the help of a microscope all their intricate beauty will be revealed. Please don't just pass them over as too small or too difficult to bother with, they are not. Anyone who feels the stirrings of 'mossology' should go to the library and borrow a book or better still go to a course run by the Field Studies

you collected them from this stream it would be more likely to be a case of kill, not cure.

Perhaps I should add a word of warning about polluted water. If you know it's polluted, keep away, but if you do fall in like I did there is no need to panic. The golden rule is don't drink it or suck your fingers after dabbling in it. If you have got an open cut or graze be sure to wash it and treat it with antiseptic when you get home. Sensible precautions, so I am going to take my own advice and get out.

Onto the opposite bank, amongst lush carpets of moss and leafy liverworts, so let's stick with them for a bit. The leafy liverworts have their 'above-ground' parts divided into stem and leaf, but if you look closely you will see that the leaves are arranged in pairs down either side of the stem. So much so that they have a flattened appearance and, looking down from above, you can always see the stem between the leaves.

Mosses are very different, their leaves are arranged in a spiral fashion around the stem so, whichever way you view them, you can only see the stem surrounded by leaves.

Just as there are two basic sorts of liverwort so too there are two basic forms of moss. This is *Mnium punctatum*, one of our most beautiful mosses. It looks like a miniature cabbage, standing upright and unbranched; this is an acrocarp. Here, on the base of the tree is another common moss and it is one of the other type, a pleurocarp. It is profusely

Council or the Adult Education Department of your local university and get down to it, I can assure you that you won't regret it.

Oh, it wasn't the base of a tree; the mosses are growing on something much more interesting – the base of a vegetable 'gonk', to be exact the Great Panicled Sedge, *Carex paniculata*. See what I mean, a short stout trunk made of thousands of dead leaves and on top a crown of living leaves, complete with triangular stems topped with masses of typical sedge flowers. What is more on the top of the 'gonk', in the midst of all the sedge leaves is a microcosm of life – mosses, both pleurocarp and acrocarp (check the characters), a leafy liverwort and *Oxalis acetosella*, Wood Sorrel, complete with its trefoil leaves some of which are already

Conocephalum conicum, **a juicy thallose liverwort growing on the clay bank of the stream.**

Vegetable 'gonks' or Greater Tussock Sedge (*Carex paniculata*) **marking out a spring area near the valley bottom** (also pictured on the front jacket).

in the crotch of an old birch tree is quite a surprise. Rosebay Willowherb is growing two metres above ground level, looking like an epiphyte! In fact, it is not quite a true epiphyte as the seeds have probably blown up here and lodged in the pad of humus which has collected in the angle of the branch; and haven't they done well. Another name for this willowherb is Fire Weed, for its natural home is open forest areas after fire. This is why it produces so many seeds, each with a silken parachute to carry it on its way to newly cleared pastures.

The gonk spring is situated on a shelf a little above the valley floor and as it is flat, it drains very slowly and hence is very wet. Round about the dominant trees are willows and that name or rather its Latin equivalent, *Salix*, is enough to make even the expert cringe. The identification of our willows is difficult and to do it properly it is a lifetime's work.

This one is easy: nice shiny, deep green leaves, and there are the catkins with the remains of 1, 2, 3, 4, 5, anthers. Without a

folded down, showing that their leaflets are capable of moving. Looking round I can see a whole army of 'gonks' marking out a large spring area in which mineral rich water is bubbling to the surface. Again, as if to prove the presence of these minerals and especially of the bases, there is a handsome plant called *Eupatorium cannabinum*, the Hemp Agrimony. The first time I ever saw that plant growing was in a very wet bit on a north facing slope on the chalk downs of Surrey; chalk is a form of limestone, rich in bases. Here, the facts fit as the water issuing from the 'gonk' spring has a pH of 7·2, just on the alkaline side of neutrality.

Again to prove that here, in the depths of the valley, the atmosphere is very humid throughout the year, the tree boles and even some of the branches, are covered with lichens. Plants which live stuck onto the outside of other plants are called epiphytes, and the damper the environment, the more epiphytes are usually found. Unfortunately, we are too close to massive sources of atmospheric pollution to be able to enjoy the full range of the arch-epiphytes – the macro-lichens. Also, this is a very young bit of woodland for we know from studying Ordnance Survey maps that less than 100 years ago it was part of a farmer's field. Despite that there are some interesting epiphyte communities to be seen and here

doubt, *Salix pentandra*. But the one next door is not so easy, everything about it says *Salix atrocinerea*, especially the rust coloured hairs on the veins of its leaves but the little auricles or ears at the base of each leaf suggest that isn't the whole story. It is, in all probability, a hybrid with the Eared Willow, *Salix aurita*, which is also growing hereabouts. No, they are not easy and to become a master of the willows you must return at each season of the year and collect them in leaf, flower and fruit.

They are, however, very important plants especially in damp habitats like this, and they are especially important to insects.

Plants with catkins are usually pollinated by the wind. Think of the clouds of yellow pollen blown from the hazel catkins early in the year. Willow catkins though, are not, and all you have to do is stand and watch on a warm sunny day. Each catkin is a hive of industry, with insects buzzing about seeking out the nectar produced by the flowers and carrying the pollen from one catkin to the next, speeding the process of pollination,

Hemp Agrimony (*Eupatorium cannabinum*)*;* **a plant that likes a little lime in its spring water.**

A living stain of iron oxide; signature of a long past and an industrial present.

fertilization and, unfortunately for budding botanists, hybridisation.

Oh, what a smashing place this is. All this diversity and yet the whole wood at this point is less than 150 metres wide.

Looking back I can see zones marked out by the different vegetation and as I retrace my steps, I will recount the series.

But first to cross the stream once more. I will choose a narrower spot. Yes, made it, home but not very dry, for here is another spring and this one doesn't look very healthy at all! It's a great soggy mass of rusty brown 'yuk' streaked with an oily opalescence. No, it's not pollution. It is one of the weirdest of all the natural phenomena here. The spring is emanating from some strata which are rich in iron. Growing in the chalybeate water are communities of very simple bacteria and bacteria-like organisms intermixed with algae and other microscopic plants. Some of the bacteria are able to use the energy of simple chemical reactions such as the oxidation of iron compounds in their life processes. These are chemosynthesisers, some of the minute proportion of life on this planet which do not depend on the energy of the sun and the process of photosynthesis. There have been organisms like these living on Earth for billions of years, and here they are still doing their own chemical thing. The thick flocculent rust is, in fact, masses of colloidal iron hydroxide, a by-product of their life processes.

It is suggested that such 'iron stains' may have helped in the Iron Age revolution which speeded early man on to destruction of Britain's woodlands and on towards the Industrial Revolution. Such iron stains

could have indicated the presence of small deposits of bog iron, enough to form the raw material for their early efforts in smelting. Who knows?

Here are my woodland zones:

Zone 1. The wettest and the closest to the stream with abundant spring water bubbling to the surface. The pH is between 6·5 and 7·0, well up towards neutrality. It is here that we find the greatest diversity of ground flora although, as we saw on the way down, it has a moderately uniform canopy domina-

Rosebay Willowherb (*Epilobium angustifolium*) **growing like an epiphyte in the fork of a birch tree.**

ted by Alder. Oh, that's nice – here around the spring head is one of the rarities of the valley and one of the more poisonous plants to be found in Britain. *Oenanthe crocata* (because it croaks you) or Hemlock Drop-wort (because it drops you). It is a member of the Umbelliferae plant family, the members of which always give themselves away by their inflorescence, that is by the way the flowers are arranged. Each flower head looks like the spokes of a wheel all arising from the same level around a stem.

This type of inflorescence is called an umbel and if the spokes are themselves branched in the same way, it is an umbel of umbels.

Zone 2. The mixed woodland, rich in trees and ferns but the soils are more acid with a pH of 5·0–6·0, which with the longer drier periods in the summer, make for a more uniform ground layer.

Zone 3. The *Sphagnum* fringe, where a peatnick like me could linger many days away.

Zone 4. Birch and Rowan and a ground flora of more acid loving plants.

Zone 5. Birch alone and little else except heathland plants and they are another story for another day.

Out into the glare of the sun and there in the distance the roofs of Chester-le-Street where lives the local expert, a retired school teacher, Tom Dunn. I must come back another day with him for only he knows the true secrets of this place: the inter-relation-ship between the plants we have seen and the insects, which he has made his life's work.

Natural history is just that, a life-long study of the inter-relations between living things. It is well worth the time and the effort, even in the most unpretentious bit of woodland.

A Coppiced Wood in Spring

Of all the products of man, coppiced woodland can be said to have improved on nature. Well, that is my opinion and I am sure that when you have read this chapter and visited one for yourself, that you will agree. Even if you don't, I am sure you will enjoy both experiences.

Coppice is a method of woodland management in which the bulk of the trees in small defined areas are cut back almost to, or even at, ground level at regular time intervals. Standard trees are left amongst the cut wood to grow to maturity. The object of this management exercise is to produce a range of timber to be used for a wide variety of jobs.

The outcome is a patchwork of woodland plots of different ages, each of which offer a different aspect of regrowth and maturity in juxtaposition to each other. Dog's Mercury, Bugle, Primroses, Bluebells, orchids and Brambles are all there, as are the full range of birds, insects and country crafts, waiting to be discovered by you.

Although coppiced management looks like an extremely ruthless way of treating a woodland it provides a rich variety of habitats for a colourful range of plants and animals. The Ash stools seen here, even though they are just above ground level, are probably over 350 years old.

Information

Coppicing is essentially a method of managing a broad-leaved woodland in order to provide a continual supply of various types and sizes of wood. In a wood, such as Bradfield, which is managed as a coppice-with-standards, there are two main types of wood: the underwood and the standard trees. The underwood is cut on a cycle which can vary from eight to ten years up to twenty-five or even thirty years, depending on the type of wood being grown and the demand. The trees are cut down to the base leaving a 'stool' from which new shoots will grow, usually as a group of straight 'poles'. When these 'poles' have grown to a suitable height they are then cut and used for a wide range of different purposes from fencing to firing wood-burning stoves. Growing up amongst the coppiced underwood are a much smaller number of 'standard' trees. These are allowed to grow naturally from seedlings and can reach anything up to two hundred years before they are cut. The timber which comes from these trees was traditionally used mainly for buildings and vehicles. Most of the work of cutting the trees is carried out in the winter months when least damage to the woodland wildlife and flora is likely to occur.

If you would like to visit a coppiced woodland or, indeed, help to manage one, you should join your local Conservation Trust as it is quite possible, especially in lowland England, that they help manage such a wood. It is a very labour intensive process and they are always glad of extra help. Some of the larger woods such as Norsey Wood, Hatfield Forest, Essex; Bradfield Woods, Suffolk; Ham Street Woods, Kent; and Hayley Woods, Cambridgeshire, have public access or open days when members of the public are shown around. Remember, these are working woodlands and produce an important crop, so please keep to the footpaths.

Cross-section of a coppiced woodland

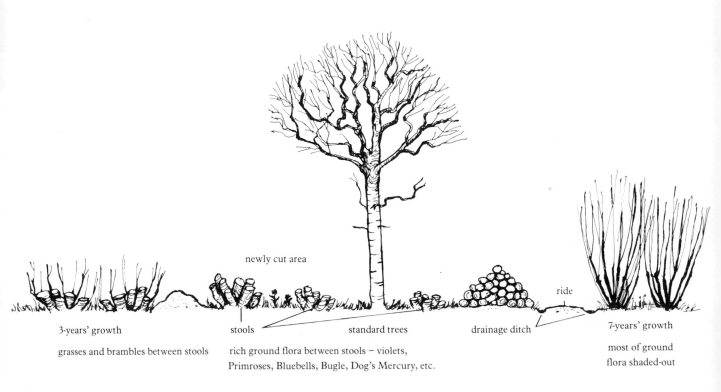

newly cut area

3-years' growth   stools   standard trees   drainage ditch   ride   7-years' growth

grasses and brambles between stools   rich ground flora between stools – violets, Primroses, Bluebells, Bugle, Dog's Mercury, etc.   most of ground flora shaded-out

Some plants and animals to look out for:

Typical trees of coppiced deciduous woodland

Sallows *Salix caprea, S. cinerea, S. atrocinerea*
Oaks *Quercus robur, Q. petraea*
Silver Birch *Betula pendula*
Downy Birch *Betula pubescens*
Alder *Alnus glutinosa*
Hornbeam *Carpinus betulus*
Hazel *Corylus avellana*
Sweet Chestnut *Castanea sativa*
Wild Cherry *Prunus avium*
Field Maple *Acer campestre*
Small-leaved Lime *Tilia cordata*
Ash *Fraxinus excelsior*

Typical spring flowers of coppiced woodland

Greater Stitchwort *Stellaria holostea*
Wood Anemone *Anemone nemorosa*
Cuckoo Flower *Cardamine pratensis*
Barren Strawberry *Potentilla sterilis*
Water Avens *Geum rivale*
Herb Bennet *Geum urbanum*
Wood Sorrel *Oxalis acetosella*
Herb Robert *Geranium robertianum*
Wood Spurge *Euphorbia amygdaloides*
Sweet Violet *Viola odorata*
Primrose *Primula vulgaris*
Bugle *Ajuga reptans*
Ground Ivy *Glechoma hederacea*
Bluebell *Endymion non-scriptus*
Ramsons *Allium ursinum*
Herb Paris *Paris quadrifolia*
Wild Arum *Arum maculatum*
Early Purple Orchid *Orchis mascula*
Dog's Mercury *Mercurialis perennis*
Lesser Celandine *Ranunculus ficaria*
Townhall Clock *Adoxa moschatellina*

Some spring woodland butterflies

Peacock *Inachis io*
Speckled Wood *Pararge aegeria*
Comma *Polygonia c-album*
Orange Tip *Anthocharis cardamines*
Brimstone *Gonepteryx rhamni*

Some typical birds of coppiced woodland

Pheasant *Phasianus colchicus*
Woodcock *Scolopax rusticola*
Wood Pigeon *Columba palumbus*
Turtle Dove *Streptopelia turtur*
Cuckoo *Cuculus canorus*
Tawny Owl *Strix aluco*
Great Spotted Woodpecker *Dendrocopos major*
Lesser Spotted Woodpecker *Dendrocopos minor*
Jay *Garrulus glandarius*
Garden Warbler *Sylvia borin*
Blackcap *Sylvia atricapilla*
Whitethroat *Sylvia communis*
Willow Warbler *Phylloscopus trochilus*
Chiffcaff *Phylloscopus collybita*
Wood Warbler *Phylloscopus sibilatrix*
Redstart *Phoenicurus phoenicurus*
Robin *Erithacus rubecula*
Nightingale *Luscinia megarhynchos*
Blackbird *Turdus merula*
Marsh Tit *Parus palustris*
Willow Tit *Parus montanus*
Blue Tit *Parus caeruleus*
Coal Tit *Parus ater*
Great Tit *Parus major*
Long-tailed Tit *Aegithalos caudatus*
Nuthatch *Sitta europaea*
Treecreeper *Certhia familiaris*
Chaffinch *Fringilla coelebs*

Typical mammals of coppiced woodland

Hedgehog *Erinaceus europaeus*
Common Shrew *Sorex araneus*
Grey Squirrel *Sciurus carolinensis*
Bank Vole *Clethrionomys glareolus*
Wood Mouse *Apodemus sylvaticus*
Common Dormouse *Muscardinus avellarnarius*
Fox *Vulpes vulpes*
Stoat *Mustela erminea*
Weasel *Mustela nivalis*
Badger *Meles meles*
Roe Deer *Capreolus capreolus*
Fallow Deer *Dama dama*

A Coppiced Wood in Spring
with Peter Fordham

On the first sunny day in May we went up to the heart of Suffolk to visit Bradfield Woods and to meet the warden, Peter Fordham, who was to show us around the reserve. The reason we had come to this wood was to see the variety of life that can be found in a coppiced broadleaved wood. We hardly expected though, the profusion of colour and sound that greeted us.

To most people a walk in a wood in spring is the time to really shake off the winter dust – the fresh green buds of the trees are bursting out, the birds seem to be singing for all their worth and the air has a freshness which is tremendously invigorating. To come across a wood with a carpet of Blue-bells is a real treat, to come across a wood carpeted with a sumptuous range of flowers from the garlic-scented Ramsons to sheets of Dog's Mercury and Bugle is something special – and this is what we found at Bradfield Woods. There are still many woods that have a good range of plants, so why don't you have a read of our walk through these woods and then go out and have a closer look at your own local wood and see what you can find.

Bradfield Woods almost didn't make it into the 1980's. The woods were purchased by the Royal Society for Nature Conservation in 1970 as a result of local efforts to prevent the wood from being totally destroyed following the clearance of a large part of a section called Monks's Park Wood

and its conversion to arable farming – a nice way of saying that it was 'grubbed-up'. Bradfield Woods, which consist of 103 acres of Felsham Hall Wood and 58 acres of Monks's Park Wood, is particularly important as it has a documented history of continuous coppicing at least since the Middle Ages, and definitely since 1252. It was initially managed by the monks of the powerful abbey of Bury St Edmunds, and the pattern of management has changed very little since then. So our walk was also a step back in time. It does not look immediately like the kind of woodland that most of us perhaps imagine an old wood should be like, as most of the trees are fairly small and in regular thickly wooded sections, here called fells. However, a closer look revealed a fascinating variety of trees. A lot of our woods were regularly coppiced until this century so it is quite possible that your neighbourhood overgrown wood will show the relict signs of the form of management that is still carried out at Bradfield.

The first thing that Peter pointed out as we left our cars and headed for the main entrance was that, although the woods are intensively managed, it is probable that there has always been woodland on the site since the last glaciation and that the variety of trees and the ground flora underline this fact. This type of woodland is known as primary woodland as opposed to secondary woodland which has grown up naturally or

Just inside the reserve is the first section, which was cut two winters ago, showing one complete year's growth. The standard trees are birches, indicating the more acid soil.

Blowing its own trumpet of beauty – a patch of Bugle (*Ajuga reptans*) enjoying the spring sunshine between the coppiced stools.

has been planted on a cleared site. The long term relationship that develops between the plants and trees in an ancient wood cannot be replaced simply by planting similar species. It is therefore extremely important that our remaining primary woodlands are protected from destruction and, wherever possible, coppiced in the traditional manner.

Peter led us up a rather muddy path to an area that had been recently coppiced. The first thing that caught the eye, unlike so many woods, was the profusion of flowers. We picked our way carefully between the coppiced stools while Peter pointed out some of the species – Sweet Violets and Bugle, some of the last of this spring's Wood Anemones, nodding Water Avens and Primroses, Dog's Mercury and, in the far corner, a swath of Bluebells. By the side of one stool was a stand of tall green Wood Spurge, a relative of the familiar Sun Spurge which can be found along our hedgerows and at the edges of fields, with its bright green flowers and leaves which completely encircle the stem.

This first area had been cut two winters ago and was showing the results of one year's full growth. Already the different rate of growth of the various trees was quite marked. The Sallow shoots were two and a half metres high while the Ash poles were still comparatively short, bending and twisting like some medusa. This apparently bizarre growth is the result of the genetic make-up of the tree, each individual showing a different pattern of growth. The Hazel shoots were also lagging behind the Sallow and were mostly two metres tall. The main standard trees in this area were Silver Birches which, together with the Bluebells indicated that the soil in this part of the wood was essentially acidic. Despite the rapid regeneration of the coppiced trees, the site was essentially open and the flowers were obviously enjoying this state. On our walk around the wood, we were to see the influence of the various degrees of tree cover on the plant life.

From this first area, we returned to the main path which was deeply rutted and wet – an indication of the poor drainage which was probably a critical factor in the wood remaining intact for so many years. The bird song was all around us as the spring sun was producing the very best from Bradfield's warblers. Willow Warblers, in particular, could be heard singing, it seemed, from almost every thicket and their cascading song was underlined by the rich tones of

unseen Nightingales. This backdrop of song remained with us for nearly the entire walk. We rounded a corner which brought us in front of what looked like a devastated area. However, Peter was quick to point out what was going on.

'Here we have an area which has been coppiced this winter and most of the wood has been sorted and moved out. So unlike the first area which had one year's growth this one, apart from the stools, has only what has grown in the last few weeks.'

The floor was carpeted with a green mantle of Dog's Mercury which was broken

by the short stumps of the coppiced trees and a few Oak standards. Some of the larger stools were Ash – these stood out from the smaller Hazel and Sallow. We had a closer look at one which had a thick covering of mosses and lichens.

'This clump, which looks like a collection of individual trees, is actually part of the same tree. As the Ash becomes older, the centre seems to divide and rot away whilst the outer layers of the tree remain vigorous. This tree here is roughly two metres in diameter and will soon have new shoots growing from the outer stumps.'

Not the kind of Ash one usually finds drawn in a reference book. Considering the great antiquity of the wood, I asked Peter how old it might be.

'This could be three hundred years old – the coppicing actually seems to extend the life of these trees, as a good age for an Ash would normally be 150 to 200 years. We have one stool here which is over six metres across and it has been estimated that it could be a thousand years old, perhaps the oldest living thing in Britain, *and* still producing a good crop of poles!'

In the centre of the clearing was an Oak

A coppiced Ash stool amongst Sallows and birch standards. These ancient stools still produce a healthy crop of poles. Notice how the Sallow poles are already much higher than the slower growing Ash, after only one year's full growth.

The Nightingale (*Luscinia megarhynchos*) is a typical bird of our traditional coppiced woods. The distribution in Britain is mainly south of a line from the Humber to the Severn. Interestingly this coincides with the area where intensive coppice-with-standards woodland management was most prevalent. They feed on the woodland floor and breed in dense thickets – a combination which suits the patchwork of recently cut woodland and impenetrable stands of poles that are found in coppiced woodland. The decline in the numbers of Nightingales in Britain over recent decades has been partly attributed to the decrease in traditional woodland management.

standard with bundles of cut wood leaning against it. These clearly showed the different rates of growth of the various wood. The Hazel was about half the height of the Sallow poles. They were all the same age as all the stools had previously been coppiced ten years ago. I asked Peter what these would be used for.

'These bundles will be used in thatching: the shorter ones will be used as thatching pins, called broaches, while the longer rods will be used to keep the thatch down, and are called spars.'

By the path was a group of Sallow poles which had been 'stripped-barked'. This was to help the wood to dry out evenly, preventing it from splitting. They had been carefully picked out for eventual use as traditional scythe handles. When I picked one up, I could feel the slight bend in the wood which gives it its distinctive action.

Each of the different coppiced trees had their own uses. The Hazel is very versatile and has a long history of use as a fencing material, for example in Hazel wattles. The larger Ash poles are used here for rake heads and teeth as well as firewood. Some of the birch is used for scythe nibs. Wood that is not used for a specific purpose is logged and sold as firewood; a product which is increasingly in demand with the recent increase in the price of oil and coal and the popularity of wood-burning stoves. The tops of the trees, which used to be sold as faggots for burning in the old kitchen stoves, are now burnt on site and the ash is sold as an excellent pottery glaze. So nothing is wasted. Burning on site can harm the ground flora, so special areas are set aside for this. Across the woodland ride was another area of coppiced woodland that looked consider-

ably different to the first two areas we had looked at. The wood was quite high and thick with straight poles. This was approximately seven years' growth. I asked Peter if this meant that it would be cut in three years' time.

'Probably, but it depends if it is mostly Hazel. If there is more Ash we would leave that for as long as 25 years, possibly for use as firewood. You have to imagine that you are looking back to medieval times here because this is the same practice as then. The main difference is that then there would probably have been twenty people working on a wood of this size, whereas now there is just myself and our woodman, Joe Bennett. However, we have a lot of voluntary help, particularly with things such as the clearing of the dead underwood before cutting. This form of woodland management is very labour intensive and we would be unable to carry it out without the help of volunteers. You cannot bring great machines into the felled areas as this would destroy not only some of the stools, which are obviously the renewable resource, but also the ground flora, which is extremely important.'

Sobered by this thought, we had a closer look at the carpets of flowers on the newly cleared site. Although we had walked no more than a hundred metres from the first area, the types of trees and flowers were already showing that we had now moved onto a more neutral soil. Here was mostly the Dog's Mercury, which seemed to be the predominant plant of the wood. The fresh green shoots of Meadowsweet, which were obviously enjoying the damp conditions, could be seen starting to rise over the Dog's Mercury. Water Avens with its shy-looking pink and orange flowers could be found in

Opposite **A newly cut area, with Ash and Hazel stools in the foreground and a standard oak in the centre of the photograph. The poles stacked against the tree will be selected for use as thatching spars and broaches.**

The distinctive four-leaved Herb Paris (*Paris quadrifolia*) **amongst Water Avens** (*Geum rivale*) **and Dog's Mercury** (*Mercurialis perennis*).

little clumps – again the dampness was the key to its presence. Peter was intent on showing me one of the specialities of the wood, and in true botanist's fashion, eyes to the ground, treading carefully, he made his way over a cleared area. After a short search, he stopped to show me what I thought at first to be another clump of Dog's Mercury. However, closer inspection revealed a delicate little green plant with four leaves surrounding a strange looking flower with greenish sepals and straggling yellow petals. This was Herb Paris, *Paris quadrifolia*. I asked Peter why such a strange looking and elusive plant should have such a name.

'If you look closely at this plant you will see that it is made up of groups of four parts. You can see that there are four main leaves in a circle around the stem, then four sepals and in between these are four thin green petals.

Now, it is said that this symmetrical arrangement resembled a traditional love knot and from this it got the name *herba paris*, which means herb of a pair. Its other common name is herb true-love, again referring back to its resemblance to a love knot. Later in the year it produces a dark berry which is poisonous but was at one time used to treat inflammation of the eyes.'

Since we were down on the floor we had a look for some more flowers and it was not long before we came upon the showy flowers of an Early Purple Orchid. This, like the Herb Paris, is an indicator of ancient woodland and is also a lime-loving plant (a calcicole). It is interesting to reflect that one of the reasons why we can use these plants as guides to the origin of a woodland is perhaps because the plants evolved in a situation where the forest cover was more or less

One of Bradfield's managed rides providing an ideal habitat for woodland insects, particularly butterflies. The ride is cut regularly to provide a range of microhabitats. The drainage ditch was probably dug during the Seventeenth or Eighteenth Century to keep the path dry.

continuous over large areas and that therefore they did not need the ability to colonise fragmented areas. So now where secondary woodland has been planted, perhaps only a short distance from ancient primary woodland, its flowers are unable to colonise these new sites. However, it is dangerous to generalise as plants behave differently in different areas. For example, here at Bradfield Woods the Bluebell is found only on the more acidic parts of the wood, whereas in western Britain its distribution is more general.

Before continuing our walk around the wood we stopped to look at the stump of an old Oak. A casual visitor might not give it a second glance but Peter knew that, like so many facets of the wood, if you knew what to look for, it had a story to tell.

'This was felled during what was prob-ably the last major clearance of the timber trees. It was brought down during the 1930's using an axe and cross cut saw. Quite often animals use these old stumps as look-out posts or feeding tables.'

The large number of rabbit droppings clearly confirmed this. There were also some broken Hazel nut shells on the surface and I asked Peter what would have left them there.

'Yes, these are very interesting. There is a clean split down the centre of the shell which means, if we can find the other half of the shell, it could be squirrel.'

We searched around and sure enough found the other half making an almost perfect match.

'The squirrel that is found here is the Grey one and you can usually tell which nuts they have eaten because they gnaw a small hole and then split the nut open with their bottom teeth, making a clean break along the line of its weakest point. Nuts that have small neat holes gnawed in them are usually the result of the work of small voles and mice and even, in woods like this, dormice.'

Suddenly the sound of birdsong was broken by a harsh bark. I turned around expecting to see somebody out walking their dog. But Peter immediately said that it sounded more like the sharp bark of a Roe Deer. Unfortunately, the deer did not show itself and we moved on deeper into the wood.

We had now come to a long straight ride with a fine springy turf. It was a lot drier than the main path and had a ditch running along each side. These had probably been dug during the Seventeenth and Eighteenth Centuries but some may be medieval. They keep the ride dry in order to help with the timber extraction. Although the main feature of the woods was obviously the trees, these ancient rides were very important in themselves and, perhaps, are the vestiges of a prehistoric grassland, older than the wood itself. Bugle was growing in patches and some Lesser Celandine, that harbinger of spring, was still in flower in some of the more sheltered places. Peter pointed out the gradation from short grass in the centre of the ride to the taller herbs on either side before the coppiced wood. The rides support a tremendous variety of flowers, which in turn help support the woodland insect population. This includes several species of butterfly, for example the Brimstone, Peacock and White Admiral. Despite the inclement spring, some butterflies were around; in particular, we came across a

Three Hazel nuts which have been broken into by three different types of mammal. (A) Has been gnawed into by a Wood Mouse (notice the outer ring of teeth marks which it makes); (B) has been gnawed into by a Bank Vole (notice the cleaner edge); (C) has been split open by a Grey Squirrel (notice the groove that it has made, it then inserts its incisors in the hole and splits open the shell).

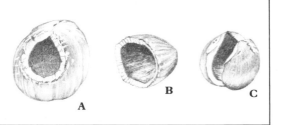

Peacock butterfly with rather shredded wings. Peter suggested that it had probably been attacked by birds. The gaudy wings with their striking eye spots would attract the birds away from the vulnerable body and so the butterfly is able to escape to see another day, although not looking at his Sunday best.

On the edge of the ride was a yellow flower looking rather like an overgrown Primrose. This was an Oxlip, a speciality of the ancient woodlands of the area. For many years it was thought to be a hybrid between the Primrose and the Cowslip, but is now recognised as a species in its own right. It has a very limited distribution in England, only being found in primary woodland on the heavy boulder clays of central East Anglia and west Cambridgeshire: yet another indication that we were in a special place.

Above **Traditional woodland harmony. Early Purple Orchid** (*Orchis mascula*) **and Dog's Mercury at the base of a three hundred year old coppiced Ash stool.**

Above left **Oxlip** (*Primula elatior*), **a speciality of the ancient woods of the boulder clays of central East Anglia and west Cambridgeshire.**

At the end of the ride which skirted the edge of the reserve we could see through the woodland edge and onto the intensively farmed Suffolk landscape. Between these arable fields with their absence of wildlife and the wood was a huge ditch with a noticeable mound on the woodland side. This was not the work of one man and his 'JCB' but rather the work of gangs of labourers under the supervision of medieval monks, as Peter pointed out.

'This is a medieval boundary bank which was constructed mainly to stop the neighbouring livestock straying into the woods and browsing off the new shoots from the coppice stools. These banks are characteristic of old coppiced woodlands and can often tell you a lot about the original boundaries or divisions within the wood. Most of them have the earth bank on the woodland side of the ditch, as here at Bradfield. At points along the bank are also old pollarded Oaks and Ash, which again clearly mark the boundary of the woodland, particularly where the coppicing goes right to the edge of the bank. Pollarding a tree means that they have been regularly cut back, not at ground level as with a coppiced tree, but at a height somewhere between two and three metres above ground to prevent livestock from reaching the new shoots. These pollarded Oaks, like the coppiced trees, can reach a great age, even though the main trunk can have rotted away, leaving holes for insects and birds.

We moved on along another muddy path. The growth alongside us, to my eye, all looked of the same age and I put it to Peter that a large part of the wood must have been cleared fairly recently.

aroma – it made walking quite a hungry business. Further on, we came to a patch that had not been coppiced for thirty years and the ground flora was noticeably different from the rich mixture of flowers that we had found on some of the more recently cut sections. Virtually the only plant that still seemed to be able to take advantage of the situation was the ubiquitous Dog's Mercury. It is probably because of the early flowering nature of the plant that it can survive under the dense cover of these older sections. However, if the wood was left to grow much longer it would itself start to deteriorate.

'If the coppice was left over forty years the Hazel, which is now overshadowed by the faster growing trees such as the Ash, would start to become shaded out and would not survive. To an extent, the fact that the Hazel comes into leaf a good deal earlier than its neighbours, like the Ash and the Oak, works to its advantage but eventually it will start to die off.'

I asked Peter if the old adage: 'The Oak before the Ash, we're in for a splash. The Ash before the Oak, we're in for a soak', had any grounding. Unfortunately he thought not, and proceeded to point out that in the woods there are individual groups of trees that regularly seem to come into leaf before others and that the timing was dependent largely on the genetic make-up of the individual trees and not the vagaries of the British climate.

We then came upon a clearing which must have been all of eight acres in extent. Peter and his woodman, with the help of teams of volunteers, had cleared it last winter and all

Bottom **The boundary bank showing the steep bank on the woodland side and the open arable land beyond. In the fore-ground is a pollarded oak marking out the boundary of the wood.**

Below **A stack of carefully selected Ash poles stripped to dry out evenly and waiting to be turned into handles for scythes** (see page 51).

'No. It has been coppiced on a fairly regular cycle, depending upon demand. We have between one and thirty-five years' growth in the wood, although we are attempting to bring some of the older areas back into the shorter cycle coppicing which is typical of the wood. Sometimes, with the older parts of the wood, as here, it can be difficult to tell the difference in age between one section and another. This is why it is helpful to coppice in one area and then move far away when you coppice the next winter so that the heights of the different parts are clearly defined.'

As we walked along between a section of 'twenty-year old' coppice, the air suddenly filled with the smell of fresh garlic. Peter pointed out a patch of Ramsons or Wild Garlic by the side of the ride. Our walk was to be continually punctuated by this glorious

Spring beauty in a coppice wood. A carpet of Ramsons or Wild Garlic (*Allium ursinum*).

that remained save the stools were the standard trees. The first clearing we had come to had mostly Silver Birch standards; here, however, the predominate tree was Oak. Great piles of cut wood lay in between these isolated Oaks. A lot of cut Ash poles would be going off to the local factory to be turned into rake heads and teeth. In front of us, were some huge Elm stools; these were larger than the Ash as they are a faster growing tree. The Oak standards were interesting as they ranged in age from comparative youngsters of thirty-five years (when the area was last cut) to about 100

years. So here a continual supply of Oak timber of a wide range of ages was clearly in evidence, demonstrating why the coppicing-with-standards form of woodland management had been so successful for so many centuries.

From this large area of recently cut woodland, we crossed over a footbridge which straddled the end of an intriguing pond. This was apparently dug at the same time as the great boundary banks. Although it is called the 'fish pond', there is currently little aquatic life in it, as it has dried out during the summer months in recent years. A new

caps were also singing and the beautiful mellow song of the Nightingale, which we first heard at the entrance to the wood, was still with us. Peter pointed out that Redstarts would soon be around, and in the evening Tawny Owls could be heard. It was pleasant to reflect that hundreds of years previously the labourers must have worked here and stopped to listen to the same sounds as we were hearing. The sense of continuity was marvellous. Practically the only difference was that, instead of simple but effective bill hooks and horses, Peter was using chain saws and tractors to cut and remove the wood.

From the pond, we moved into Monks's Park Wood, a deer park maintained by the monks. This part had been coppiced three winters previously and the ground flora was different again from the other sites we had looked at. Here there were tall woodland grasses growing up between the stools; walking was much more difficult as brambles were also covering the ground in places. However, as the trees continue to grow and start to shade out more and more of the

An area of two years' growth showing the increasing presence of grasses around an Ash stool.

sluice has been installed which, it is hoped, will improve the situation. It is a haven for frogs and it is not unusual to come across them on some of the wetter parts of the woods. In fact, there are small natural pools throughout the woods which have formed in depressions which, it has been suggested, have remained the same since post-glacial times.

Whilst we were looking down at the pond, the sound of bird song was all around us. A Whitethroat was singing from a nearby thicket, rising into a brief song flight before disappearing into the trees. Black-

plants beneath them, the less shade tolerant flowers and grasses die back. So the balance is restored and the trees' growth does not suffer from this constantly changing pattern of plants around them. Peter pointed out an area in front of us, which had a thick cover of trees, as a piece of secondary woodland called 'Hewitt's Meadow'. It had a boundary ditch around it and was traditionally an area kept aside for deer and was still open until 1900 when it was allowed to become overgrown. These meadows were used as deer parks and are typical of medieval woodland. They were also called launds.

An area of three years'
growth and grasses,
rushes, brambles and
thistles have moved in
to dominate the
ground flora.

We then threaded our way through the
cut stools to an adjoining area. Walking
between the stools was not easy. There were
two reasons for this: firstly, they were not in
the neat regimented rows that we associate
with modern coniferous plantations;
secondly, all the newly cut stools had nasty
sharp edges. Peter told me that this was
intentional, as it was important that the
poles were cut off at an acute angle so the
rainwater could run off them easily. If they
were cut level, the stool would soon
become rotten. Eventually we came out into
a fell that had been cut that winter, and I
asked Peter how they moved the timber out
as it was obviously so difficult to maneouver
around in the wood.

'In the old times, the cut wood had to be
moved out to the main rides by hand; this
was usually done by bundling it up and
carrying it out on the backs of the woodmen,
which meant that it was hard and time
consuming work. It was then loaded onto a
horse-drawn cart. Today, we make racks
into the fell and take out the wood with a
tractor and trailer.'

As we walked along, we picked out the
different species of tree that we passed –
there were Ash and Hazel, Birch and Sallow
mostly in the coppiced areas with the larger
standard Oaks. There were coppiced Alder
in the wetter patches and Peter told me that
there were Small-leaved Limes in another
part of the wood. Old Wild Cherries were
growing along the uncut edges of the fells,
together with Hawthorns. We came upon a
Field Maple which was chiefly recognisable
by its corky bark and hawthorn-like leaves. I
put it to Peter that this diversity was surely
exceptional, as most people consider coppiced woodland to be rather poor in tree
species.

'In parts of the Midlands and East Anglia,
these old coppiced woodlands are still surviving and generally have a good variety of
species. In some areas, there are large woods
which consist of coppiced Sweet Chestnut.
These woods were introduced mostly after
the Fifteenth Century, and can be found
particularly in east Essex, Kent and Sussex.
Sweet Chestnut is still used in these areas
for fencing posts and hop poles.

Walking back through the wood with its
sudden changes of view from dense thickets
to open fells carpeted with spring flowers,
Peter and I talked about the importance of
maintaining the tradition of these woods
which were sadly now an oasis for wildlife
amidst a vast monolithic arable landscape.
And yet the wood is not a museum piece. It
is a working vital place which still caters
for the needs of some of the local industries.
Before we left, I helped Peter load up some
Ash poles for the roof of a mock Saxon
village house which was being constructed
nearby. It would be nice to think that poles
would have been cut from the same site for
actual Saxon huts all those centuries ago,
and that the unbroken continuity of use
will carry on for as long again into the future.

The Rake Factory at Welnetham, Suffolk. The continued presence of this small factory producing scythe-handles, rakes and mallets has provided an example of the traditional symbiotic relationship between woodland management and local rural industry. Opposite bottom **An Ash pole being turned down by hand to produce a scythe handle.** Top **Ash poles on a bending rack destined to be scythe handles. Soft technology for a hard job.** Bottom **The finished product – two perfect scythe handles.**

A Scottish Pine Wood

The Rothiemurchus Forest or The Blackwoods of Rannoch are as much a feature of Scotland as are the glens, the bienns and the burns. They are the two largest remnants of the great Caledonian pine forest which once covered much of the Highlands. There are many more much smaller relicts of this forest clinging to the more inaccessible spots of the glens and this walk visits one of these near Speyside. There you can see for yourself the structure of the forest dominated by true Scots Pine, the open floor of which provides a home for many members of the Heather family and for a diverse cross-section of the wild flowers and wildlife of the Highlands. A trip to one of these Scottish woods is a must in the apprenticeship of any natural historian.

A part of the Caledonian pine wood in a Speyside mountain pass.

Information

Coniferous woodland, that is woods largely composed of trees belonging to the Gymnosperms (Yew, Juniper, cedars, pines, spruces, larches, etc.), is largely planted or naturalised in Britain. The more rapid growth of these trees and their uniformly straight trunks mean that they are a more profitable crop than our native hardwoods. It is not unusual to find old coppice-with-standards woodland totally replaced with modern conifer plantations. The ability of these trees to grow on poor soils has meant that in some upland regions they have been extensively planted. This preference for coniferous plantations has dramatically altered the landscape in recent years, replacing open moorland or species rich broad-leaved woodland with large areas of monospecific woodland. This means that it is now increasingly important to preserve our existing more traditional woodland types. However, the new plantations are not wholly bad from an ecological point of view as, with considerate management, in time they will become more varied and support greater number of species. The rich and varied ecosystem of our relict native pine woods in Scotland testifies to this. It is worth reflecting, though, that these pine woods have a long ecological history in that region, and therefore have a wide range of animals dependent upon them, whereas the dense plantations of Norway and Sitka Spruce, for example, have few animals in Britain that are adapted to feed on them. This extensive planting with alien species has led to problems with insect pests, as some species such as the Pine Beauty Moth have taken advantage of this vast new source of food and, unconstrained by any natural mechanisms of control, have defoliated large areas. To counteract this, some areas are now sprayed with insecticides from the air, such practices affecting other insects and the birds that feed on them. Some mammals, however, have benefited from the dense cover provided by the new plantations. Deer, in particular, have taken advantage of the protection to expand their populations unmolested.

Some plants and animals to look out for:

Plants

Juniper *Juniper communis*
Scots Pine *Pinus sylvestris* var. *scotica*
Silver Birch *Betula pendula*
Downy Birch *Betula pubescens*
Aspen *Populus tremula*

In many parts of Britain introduced species of softwood tree are extensively planted with Scots Pines. These include:
Norwegian Spruce *Picea abies*
Lodge-pole Pine *Pinus contorta*
Douglas Fir *Pseudotsuga menziesii*
Sitka Spruce *Picea sitchensis*
Corsican Pine *Pinus nigra*
Larch *Larix decidua*

Common Sundew *Drosera rotundifolia*
Wood Sorrel *Oxalis acetosella*
Common Wintergreen *Pyrola minor*
Serrated Wintergreen *Orthilia secunda*
Heather *Calluna vulgaris*
Bell Heather *Erica cinerea*
Cross-leaved Heath *Erica tetralix*
Bilberry *Vaccinum myrtillus*
Cowberry *Vaccinum vitis-idaea*
Bearberry *Arctostaphylos uva-ursi*
Crowberry *Empetrum nigrum*
Chickweed Wintergreen *Trientalis europaea*
Common Cow-wheat *Melampyrum pratense*
Butterwort *Pinguicula vulgaris*
Bracken *Pteridium aquilinum*
Mosses and lichens
  Ptilium crista-castrensis
  Rhyfidiadephus loreus

Birds

Capercaillie *Tetrao urogallus*
Great Spotted Woodpecker *Dendrocopos major*
Tree Pipit *Anthus trivialis*
Goldcrest *Regulus regulus*
Spotted Flycatcher *Muscicapa striata*
Redstart *Phoenicurus phoenicurus*
Ring Ouzel *Turdus torquatus*
Coal Tit *Parus ater*
Crested Tit *Parus cristatus*
Blue Tit *Parus caeruleus*
Treecreeper *Certhia familiaris*
Chaffinch *Fringilla coelebs*
Siskin *Carduelis spinus*
Redpoll *Carduelis flammea*
Crossbill *Loxia curvirostra*
Willow Warbler *Phylloscopus trochilus*

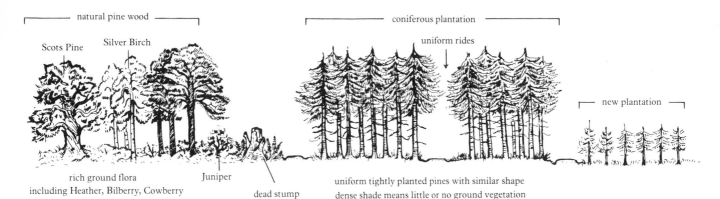

natural pine wood — coniferous plantation

Scots Pine Silver Birch

uniform rides

new plantation

rich ground flora
including Heather, Bilberry, Cowberry

Juniper

dead stump

uniform tightly planted pines with similar shape
dense shade means little or no ground vegetation

Mammals

Red Squirrel *Sciurus vulgaris*
Fox *Vulpes vulpes*
Rabbit *Oryctolagus cuniculus*
Pine Marten *Martes martes*
Stoat *Mustela erminea*
Weasel *Mustela nivalis*
Wild Cat *Felis silvestris*

Red Deer *Cervus elaphus*
Roe Deer *Capreolus capreolus*

Insects

Pine Beauty *Panolis flammea*
Pine bark beetle
Scotch Argus *Erebia aethiops*
Wood Ant *Formica rufa*

Sites

The following is a selection of coniferous woods and plantations from throughout Britain. Those in England and Wales are planted, although some pine woods such as those on heaths in southern England are partly self-seeded and many appear to be natural. The Forestry Commission have many Forest Parks where facilities such as picnic-sites, information centres and waymarked walks are provided for visitors.

Beinn Eighe, Ross-shire. National Nature Reserve. Contains natural Caledonian pine wood as well as modern plantations. Animal life includes Red Squirrel, Wildcat and Pine Marten. Nature Trails.

Glen Affric, Highlands. Highland glen including Caledonian pine wood. Waymarked forest walks.

Glen More Forest Park, Highlands. Extensive Forestry Commission area centred around Loch Morlich with both new plantations and areas of relict Caledonian pine wood, such as Ryvoan Pass (managed by Scottish Wildlife Trust).

Cairngorms, Highlands. National Nature Reserve. Large area containing extensive pine woods and plantations on lower slopes. Loch an Eilein in the Rothiemurchus Estate has a NCC nature trail.

Rannoch Forest, Tayside. Area with natural pine and birch forest as well as extensive Forestry Commission plantations. Waymarked forest walks.

Argyll Forest Park, Strathclyde. Extensive Forestry Commission Park amidst rugged scenery of West Highlands. Forest walks.

Queen Elizabeth Forest Park, Strathclyde. Forestry Commission Park including Loch Lomondside and part of the Trussocks. Forest walks.

Galloway Forest Park, Galloway. Forestry Commission Park, including Glen Trool. Forest walks.

Border/Kielder Forest Park, Borders/Northumberland. Forestry Commission Park including extensive upland areas. Many forest walks.

Hamsterley Forest, Durham. Forestry Commission managed mixed woodland, including extensive plantations. Forest waymarked walks and information centre.

Grizedale Forest, Cumbria. Forestry Commission managed woodland with oaks as well as larch, spruce and pine plantations. Nature Trails, visitor centre.

Clwyd Forest, Clwyd. Forestry Commission managed woods with extensive plantations. Waymarked forest walks.

Snowdonia Forest Park, Gwynedd. Extensive area of forest including large areas of Forestry Commission spruce and pine plantations. Numerous forest walks, including walk for disabled at Garth Falls.

Thetford Chase, Norfolk. Former breckland area now extensively planted with conifer plantations managed by Forestry Commission. Red Squirrels and Crossbills can be seen. Many forest walks and information centre.

Kingley Vale, Hampshire. National Nature Reserve. Yew woods on chalk valley; some of the trees are over 500 years old. One of the best examples of this woodland type in Europe. Nature Trail.

New Forest, Hampshire/Dorset. Extensive area of mixed woodland managed by Forestry Commission. Includes areas of pine, larch, spruce plantation. Naturalised pines in more open areas on heaths and valley bogs. Whole area of immense interest.

A Scottish Pine Wood
with Alastair Sommerville

For many people the thought of a walk in a pine forest probably conjures up a picture of long straight rides between densely packed acres of conifers. The green sward of the regularly cut ride contrasting with the all pervasive shade under the trees where, perhaps, only bracken and a few mosses manage to survive. Although some of the conifer plantations can provide, when thoughtfully managed, an interesting habitat for a reasonable range of plants and animals, there is no comparison between these and the wealth of life to be found in the Caledonian pine forests of the Scottish Highlands. To find out about the ecology of the Scots Pine, *Pinus sylvestris*, and the associated wildlife to be found in these relict forests, we travelled up to Glen More for a walk through a mountain pass under the management of the Scottish Wildlife Trust. Their Conservation Officer, Dr Alastair

Sommerville, was our guide for the day.

It had been raining heavily most of the morning so the air was clear and fresh when we started out amidst the familiar landscape of forest tracks and rows of regimented conifers. However, as we approached the pass the view began to open out and soon we were looking across a totally different landscape. Great pines, some isolated and others in small groups, were scattered in front of us. Most of them were growing on the steep sides of the valley in-between drifts of scree. The 'forest' was surprisingly open and in the flat valley bottom there were large areas with only the occasional stunted pine. Whilst we were standing at the entrance to the pass, I asked Alastair about the background to the forest.

'This general area is known as the Glen More Forest and this particular patch here is a relict of the Caledonian pine wood. The

Real Scots Pine (*Pinus sylvestris* var. *scotica*) **growing as nature planted them; a tumble of shapes and sizes amidst a glorious landscape.**

most important thing about the wood is that it dates from something like 9000 to 10000 years ago. Now, because of the known human history of this area it is safe to say that it was relatively untouched until approximately 300 years ago. And even then it was never managed in a way like the woodlands of England. So in a sense these parts that are still in a semi-natural state, like here, rank amongst the most original woodland habitats in the whole of Britain. This site was exploited primarily for its timber and the large trees were selectively felled leaving only the saplings. It is said that they dammed the valley bottom and gradually flushed the timber down to the River Spey over a number of seasons. However, this felling does not entirely explain the open nature of some of the site and as we go along we will see that there are certain conditions which prevent the continued growth of the pine forest.

The Glen More Forest was bought by the Forestry Commission in 1926 and is now designated as a forest park. Because of the specialist management required to keep this pass as part of the Caledonian pine wood, the Scottish Wildlife Trust signed an agreement in 1976 to manage the 300 or so acres.'

We made our way along and into the pass. Before we reached the main area we had to go through a high deer fence. This kept the deer out of the main Forestry plantations but it meant that the pass was unprotected. A feature we were to discover played an important part in the development of the trees. The first thing that struck me was that unlike the planted pine woods of southern England, the ground cover was thick with plants – so thick it was positively dangerous to wander from the path as all the boulders and gullies were hidden beneath this mass of shrubs and heaths. We arrived under the

spreading boughs of an old pine, looking, again, quite unlike even the isolated pines with their tall trunks and high canopy of branches, that are to be found on the sandy soils of East Anglia and southern England. I asked Alastair how old these trees might be.

'Well, they are probably of the order of 100 to 150 years old although there is a possibility that some could be as old as 300 years, dating back to the clearance.'

We are used to associating Scots Pine with artificial planting so it was interesting to see how the pines had fared under these more natural conditions.

'Scots Pine like to grow on well-drained soils. It won't grow in water-logged soil and here you can see that the flat valley bottom has fewer trees growing on it. Also, those

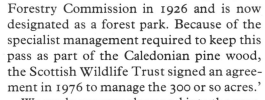

A nearby plantation of Scots Pine, each one selected to give uniform, fast growth.

The trees of the old Caledonian woods have not been selected and, as a result, show a much wider genetic variation than those in a modern commercial plantation. These illustrated here show the tremendous differences in shape, even in trees from the same valley, from ones with large branches spreading out almost from the base of the trunk to high conical-shaped trees.

that have managed to survive, are comparatively stunted. It is on the steeper slopes and on heaps of gravel, pebbles and boulders, left by the Ice Age, that the trees really come into their own. This ability to grow successfully on this type of soil, which is poor in nutrients, gives them the edge over other tree species. This is also why they have been so successful in plantations on poor sandy soils like the brecklands in East Anglia. One important reason why the tree can thrive, whereas others appear to be unable to survive, is that they have a mycorrhizal association with a fungus. The fungus, which forms an absorbing sheath over the roots of the tree, allows access to nutrients in the soil, which would otherwise be unavailable to the tree. The fungi particularly like the acid conditions that develop on these sandy, gravelly soils.

'Looking up at this tree beside us we can see the chief characteristics of the Scots Pine. First, there is, of course, this bark that

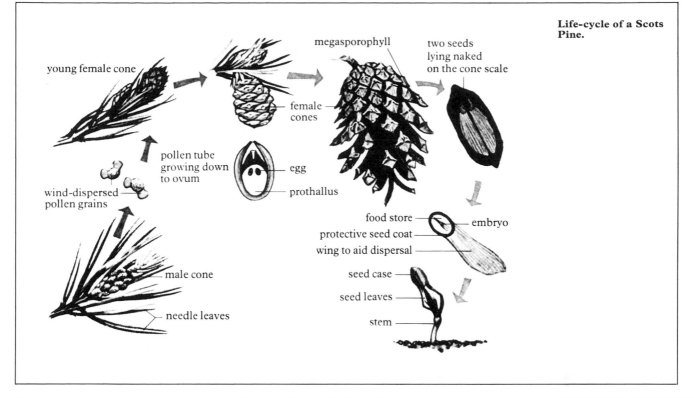

Life-cycle of a Scots Pine.

young female cone

megasporophyll

two seeds lying naked on the cone scale

female cones

pollen tube growing down to ovum

egg

prothallus

wind-dispersed pollen grains

food store — embryo

protective seed coat

wing to aid dispersal

male cone

seed case

seed leaves

needle leaves

stem

the mature trees always have. It is made up of great plates which are greyish in colour with deep fissures between them. The branches have this rather flakey bark and show up a distinctive reddish-pink colour. If you look around you will notice that some of the trees are tall with a broad crown whereas others are much more squat and have branches coming out very low down on the trunk. None of the trees have been brashed – the forester's term for cutting the low branches off in order to get a nice straight trunk – so here you have a purely natural shape to the trees. Furthermore, because this is not a commercial plantation the seeds which have germinated have not been selected by man so there is a much wider range of genetic variation. If this was a plantation the forester would have selected out the seed from the trees with the straightest trunks and hence the pines would all look more or less the same.

'It is interesting coming up today from Edinburgh because the trees here are possibly three weeks or more behind in this year's growth than those further south. Now, if you look at this sapling here, you can see that the branches are borne in whorls around the stem. So you can see that there is a stretch of trunk and then a ring of branches, then another stretch of trunk and a ring of branches and so on. Each of these intervals shows, in fact, a year's growth. So

if you find a pine and can locate the true ground level, just by counting the number of rings of branches you can age the tree. This method of whorled growth also continues along the branches giving the pine its characteristic shape as opposed to, say, a spruce. If you look at the end of a branch on a mature tree you will find the needles again in rings and borne on little stalks called dwarf shoots. At this time of the year you can clearly see the bright green shoot which is this year's growth. The needles behind this shoot are last year's, then behind that are the slightly darker needles which belong to the year before. Beyond that, going back four years, we can see that the needles are starting to fall off. If we take it further back, the needles have gone. So the idea that conifers do not lose their needles really applies only to the fact that they do not lose them all at once every autumn. They drop off eventually and three to five years is as long as they are likely to last.

'An interesting thing about the shoots themselves is that they are day-length dependent. They start to grow when the days begin to increase in length, but before they will do this they need to be chilled by the cold winter. They elongate rapidly in mid-spring and have stopped growing by mid-July. By this time a bud is forming at the tip of the shoot, and this is laying down the food reserves for next year's growth.

Although pines do not drop all their leaves in the autumn, as in deciduous trees, they do eventually lose them. This pine twig shows three years' needles borne in whorls around the shoot. Those at the base will soon start to fall.

'The ends of some of the shoots will have two little female cones on them and these will be pollinated by the male "flowers" further back at the base of the shoot. The pollen is wind blown and, in order that there is cross-fertilization between trees, the male parts on any specific tree ripen before the female cones so that their pollen is blown onto another tree where the female cones might be ripe.

'If we look at a branch, we can see clearly that the cones take several years to grow. There don't seem to be many cones about but here's one . . . Now, this one is last year's cone which is still tightly closed but if we were to look inside it, under each scale we would find two winged seeds. Behind these cones further up the branch are the previous year's cones which are the familiar woody texture and are now open having released their seeds. Therefore you can have cones up to three year's old on a branch. The pine seed is packed full of goodness and they are an important food source for the squirrels and some of the birds that live in the woods. We shall have a look at those a little later.

'The story of the life-cycle of the pine is far from over, as these wind blown seeds have to be able to find a suitable patch of ground to root themselves. If we look around we can see that there is an immediate problem. This layer of vegetation which carpets the ground is very thick. If I put my hand down through it you can see that it is, what, half a metre or more, before I reach the soil. Then the soil itself is pretty superficial. So, as far as the pine is concerned, when the seeds fall onto this bushy mat they will need to put out roots over half a metre long before then can reach any nutrients. So not surprisingly, if we look around we can see that there are no young seedling pines at all. When we wander on we'll see that the young pines grow well only on the bare soil patches. This problem, depending on how you look at it, shows how the natural woodland works or the way that it has to be managed to ensure continuous generations of pines.'

The ground cover was obviously an important feature of this part of the valley so I asked Alastair to identify its main plant species.

'The main plants here are Heather or Ling, *Calluna vulgaris*, and two species of *Vaccinium*, Bilberry, *V. myrtillus*, with its rather delicate leaves, and Cowberry, *V. vitis-idaea*, which has glossy leaves. The Bilberry has greenish-red flowers and later

The floor of the valley showing its open nature with the dense ground cover of Heather, Juniper, Bilberry and Cowberry.

on in the year it will have black berries with a distinctive purplish bloom. Whilst the Cowberry has lovely pinkish bell-shaped flowers with the petals turned up at the edges and a bright red berry. Both the berries are edible.

'Another important species here is the Juniper, *Juniperus communis*, which is really a shrub and although it is growing to just over a metre here, it can grow, particularly in sheltered conditions, to a height of three metres. The Bilberry and the Heather, in particular, are typically associated with pine woods on these acid soils. Underneath these plants is a dense growth of mosses which thrives in the sheltered humid atmosphere underneath the shrub layer.

'There is not a huge range of plants because of these very acid soil conditions which, in this case, is the result mostly of weathered granite. We might see twenty species of plant which can grow successfully here, but not many more than that. Interestingly there is an area which we will come to which is lime-rich and this shows the dramatic change in the vegetation that you get when the soil is enriched.'

We headed on up the pass and could now clearly see the classic U-shaped profile of a glaciated valley. Across the bottom there were a number of obvious ridges; these were moraines left by interruptions in the gradual retreat of the glacier. The floor of the valley, where we could see it between the thick mantle of heather, was covered in loose boulders and gravel left by the glacier.

By the side of the path we came upon a wonderfully gnarled birch, its branches festooned with lichens. The twisted branches and its stooping nature seemed to imply that it was very old but Alastair pointed out that they seldom live above sixty or seventy years. However, the birch is an important tree as it is usually the first to colonise a site, being able to tolerate the harshest conditions. Certainly compared with some of the pampered birches in the south of England, this one looked as though it had had a pretty hard time. The lichen growth indicated the high humidity of the valley and also the clean air. On one of the higher branches there was a dense mass of twigs. This was 'witch's broom', which is caused by a bacterial infection which stimulates the plant into abnormal growth.

We then came across a pine close to the path which had its roots partly exposed. They appeared to stretch a long way from

Above **Juniper** (*Juniperus communis*). **Its berry-like fruits (remember, they cannot be berries as the Juniper is not a flower-bearing plant; it is a conifer) are used by humans for flavouring gin.**

Left **Bilberry** (*Vaccinium myrtillus*) **in its early summer form, complete with flowers. In the autumn the leaves are shed, but before they fall, they change through a wonderful range of colours.**

Cowberry (*Vaccinium vitis-idaea*). **Another member of the Heath family. Unlike its cousin, the Bilberry, it has glossy evergreen leaves and a bright red berry.**

Not much of a forest, for here at the head of the pass the Scots Pines grow wherever they can, even on the stabilised scree. The flat bottom of the valley, also has few trees as the pines prefer a well-drained soil, also this area was thoroughly cleared by man.

the base of the tree. I asked Alastair if this was characteristic.

'Typically the Scots Pine does form a broad plate of roots like this. They don't have a deep tap root like an Oak, for example, and this means they are highly suited to this type of terrain with its shallow soil. But it also means that they are not terribly well anchored and pines planted in plantations can suffer from "wind throw". This is because, unlike these trees which manage to balance the ratio of the root area to the crown, in a tightly packed plantation the balance can often be wrong and when the wind gets in they can all come down.

'Over here, by the path, you can see the importance of bare ground for the pine seedlings. We have a semi-natural situation where a tree has been uprooted and there is an artificial one, the edge of the path. Both these patches of bare soil are just the sort of place where a seedling can get going. Happily there are a number of baby pines sprouting up. So you can imagine at the right time of the year the whole ground is saturated by these little seeds which have fluttered down from the open cones. Some have been stopped by the heather or moss and come to nothing, whilst other are able to take root on this bare ground.

A Silver Birch, one of the arch-colonisers of these poor infertile soils. The abundant lichens obscuring the bark indicate the damp unpolluted upland atmosphere.

A mature Scots Pine with its root system partially exposed. This typically grows as a 'plate' extending over the surface of the bedrock, seeking out water and minerals, as well as anchoring the tree.

We were now right into the pass and had arrived next to a broad flat region in the valley bottom. This was one of the sections that had been dammed up when they had been flushing the cut timber down the valley all those years ago. There were noticeably fewer trees here even on the moraine hummocks which were presumably well-drained. Alastair pointed out that it was the former human interference that was the vital factor.

'I imagine that the central valley was totally cleared as they probably cut down even the saplings to make huts and fires for the forestry workers. Then, with the in-crease in light, the heather would have moved in forming a thick cover and any seeds drifting in from the valley sides would have been unable to get a foothold.'

On the bank of the path we came across another plant which, although looking like a cross between the Heather and the Bilberry, was, in fact, related to neither – Crowberry, *Empetrum nigrum*, a member of the Empetraceae. It was another specialist plant of these acid soils. Nearby, we found a member of the Wintergreen family – the Common Wintergreen, *Pyrola minor*. The wintergreens are typical flowers of these pine woods and, as their name suggests, they

A stag Red Deer bellowing in the rutting season. These handsome animals come down from the mountain tops during the winter and cause serious damage by browsing off the new shoots of the pines.

these very obvious signs of grazing. All the forks in its growth are the result of the leading shoot being nibbled off. Although pines don't have the powers of regeneration, in the sense that if you cut them down they would put up new shoots like a coppiced tree, if the leading shoot is knocked off a new shoot can take over from a ring of buds around its base. So they can still keep going, despite being nibbled back. The result at this stage looks something like a bonsai tree. We are outside the deer fence here and the grazing pressure is one of the main management problems, even in summer. In winter, a lot of Red Deer will come down off the hills and graze on these small pines, as they are about the only thing that sticks up above the snow. So it is a real problem. In order to ensure a future woodland, you either have enough trees so that some will survive despite this grazing or you must actually protect the trees in some way, either by culling the deer or fencing them out, or even by protecting the individual trees.'

We made our way back down to the path and almost immediately came upon another plant of the heath family. This was Bearberry which has the wonderful latin name of *Arctostaphylos uva-ursi*. Alastair told us some more about it.

'It is a typically creeping plant with shiny green leaves and pink flowers and this is just

have evergreen leaves. This area is particularly favoured in that four of the five British species have been recorded. Later in our searches we were fortunate enough to find the delicate Serrated Wintergreen, *Orthilia secunda*, with its spike of yellow flowers with their protruding stamens.

At this point, having explained the absence of any pine seedlings in the dense heather, Alastair noticed that just above the path was an area that seemed to contradict this. So we clambered up to have a closer look.

'This tree here sticking up above the heather, although it is only just over a metre high is, in fact, quite old. I would say looking at the branching that it is something like twenty-five years old. So to explain this patch of trees, assuming they are all roughly the same age, we have to think of something that happened a quarter of a century ago. Now, if you look at the heather you will notice that it is not quite as rank as in the surrounding areas and, I would imagine that this was the site of a fire all those years ago. This gave the seedlings a chance to root and since then the heather has closed back in again. This, together with grazing by deer, has retarded the growth of the tree. Now it is above the heather it should start to shoot more vigorously. I can see some that, if you look at the interval between the branching of last year and the year before, are clearly doing better already. Our tree here shows

the sort of site to find it – a steep open bank. This one is really keeping close to the ground and is only sending up a couple of shoot above the mat. Nowadays it is found frequently in artificial situations such as roadsides. Naturally it would be found on a rocky surface, such as a scree slope, where it can root in a hollow and then spread out

and exploit another area where it could not normally grow.'

Along the bank from the Bearberry we found some Common Cowheat, *Melampyrum pratense*, another plant which grows in acid woodlands. Although Cowheat is fairly widespread throughout Britain, this particular mixture of plants and especially the wintergreens are fairly specific to these northern pine woods.

The structure of the soil which is such a controlling factor in the distribution of the plant life could be clearly seen at this point as the path had eaten in to the side of the valley. I asked Alastair to describe it.

'This cross-section shows the typical moraine material – gravelly-sand and broken down granite with rounded boulders left by the glaciers. The soil which develops on this material is free draining and consists of a thin layer of humus on top and below that, where the soil is leached, is sterile sand and gravel. The nutrients that have been removed from this layer are then redeposited about half a metre below the surface as an iron pan. The whole structure is known as a podsol. This means that, not only have you got these very acid layers near the surface, but, because of the iron pan there is no interconnection between these layers and the sub-soil. It is to get over this problem in many upland wet areas that the forester when he is planting will deep plough to break through the iron pan. This deep ploughing also produces a well-drained soil in the up-turned sod for the young tree and creates drainage channels to take away any excess water.'

We were now at the far end of the pass and the trees were becoming noticeably thinner on the ground. I asked Alastair why the few individuals were left behind, whilst all those around them had presumably been felled and carted away.

'I think it is just chance. Probably at the time the area was felled they were just weedy saplings and were simply not worth bothering with. In fact, many of the fragments of old wood elsewhere in Scotland consist of relatively small groups of isolated trees of one age which were obviously rejected at the time when the others were felled. Unfortunately, they cannot regenerate because the ground cover underneath is now unfavourable and that will be the end of the wood unless somebody does something about it.

'People are hoping that this particular

Bearberry (*Arctostaphylos uva-ursi*) sprawling in typical fashion down a slope. When you find one, take a close look at its flowers. This plant is a hive of activity at flowering time – nectar is secreted from a ring around the ovary and pollen is shaken from the pores in the anthers.

Despite its small size this Scots Pine is probably over twenty-five years old. It has been stunted as a result of browsing by deer but hopefully it will eventually grow out of their reach.

Soil is a product of the bedrock and of weathering by climate, plants and animals alike. Here in the cool, wet upland environment iron and other minerals are leached down through the soil profile to form this distinctive iron pan, which is so hard that it forms a barrier both to tree roots and rainwater.

Opposite **The base of a scree slope with a host of animals and plants that like 'having their feet wet': – bog mosses; two insectivorous plants, Sundew and Butterwort; and a frog.**

forest will spread and eventually join up with another area over the hill. Ironically, the path with its bare soil looks as though it is the key to this regeneration. Up until now our management has consisted of taking stock of the trees – what ages they are and how they are distributed over the reserve. We have now to work out a technique of ensuring a succession of young trees. We have seen that bare ground is an answer and, in some areas, we will look at the possibility of selective burning of the heather. But then, as we have seen, the grazing is also a problem.'

We crossed over to the other side of the valley. While we had been looking at all the flora, the profusion of birds moving around above us had not gone unnoticed. There was clearly quite a healthy community of birds associated with these stately pines. We had our binoculars with us and under Alastair's expert guidance we began to piece together the species that were busy feeding.

'That's a Willow Warbler . . . the small greenish-grey bird. But most of them are Coal Tits, which are really specialist birds of pine trees although they are found throughout Britain. They have small beaks which are very effective at poking for insects in-between the pine needles and cones. All that churring is coming from a family of Wrens . . . see them moving low amongst that fallen branch. There are some real specialities in these woods that we might see – Crossbills and Siskins and, perhaps, the Crested Tit, which in Britain is almost confined to these ancient Scottish pine woods. There are also Capercaillie in this area but unfortunately not in this particular wood. These handsome birds are generally typical

of these Scottish pine woods and also some of the new plantations. But one of the important things here, as regards the animal life, is that, unlike the plantations, you have not only a good age range in the trees but also there are rotten pine stumps and decaying trunks on the ground which provide important habitats for the insect and bird life.'

We moved along between the pines occasionally scanning the tops of the trees for birds. Nearer the ground we saw some more familiar birds – Robins and Blackbirds; here in their natural open wood habitat. Then we heard a different sound – a short thrush-like warble – obligingly its owner soon came into view. It was a handsome cock Redstart, his bright red and blue plumage showing up beautifully. I had always associated this bird with mature broad-leaved woodlands but they seemed very much at home here. Alastair explained.

'They are a typical old woodland bird. They like these old pines because of the variety of niches available. They would use the holes in the rotten wood for nesting and also these provide a good place for abundant insect food. The canopy of the trees is also rich in insects. Caterpillars would probably suit the Redstarts and the smaller prey will be taken by the Coal Tits, for instance. Amongst the heather there are also various prey species such as the Heath Moth.

'I am sure that some of the small birds flying around between the tops of the pines are Siskins. They are small green and yellow finches which are particularly adept at getting food from the cones. The other finch that breeds here is the Crossbill, which, true to its name, has a bill where the mandibles cross over each other. It uses this extraordinary adaptation to prize open the pine cones and extract the seeds. Interestingly, they are one of our earliest nesting birds – you can find them sitting on their nest even in the snow. They do this so that they are feeding their young when the pine cone seeds are mature, which is usually early in the spring.' As we continued our walk Alastair told us about some of the mammals that could be found in the woods.

'One creature we must not forget is the Red Squirrel. Again this is a real specialist of conifer woods. It does also live in deciduous woods, but the current theory is that when the Grey Squirrel moves in, it is so good at exploiting these woods that it fares a lot better than the Red Squirrel. There is also the suggestion that Red Squirrels can suffer from a virus disease like myxomatosis and, if they are put under stress, they can actually die of this latent virus that they have in their bodies. The point is that if they are in coniferous woodlands, they should be safe, because the Grey Squirrel is not as competent at coping with the food sources. Eventually, what might happen is that the Red Squirrel will be only found in coniferous woods or mixed woods with lots of conifers. Here, however, they are abundant.

'Two other interesting mammals that are found in this region, although we are unlikely to see them, are the Pine Marten and the Wild Cat. Both have benefited from the reafforestation and also from the relative lack of persecution this century, and we are now hearing of sightings of both these animals right down in the central belt of Scotland.'

A sudden sharp bark startled us and we quickly scanned the opposite side of the valley where the noise had come from. It was a buck Roe Deer, which we could just make out by a scree slope. But then we lost it, which is so often the way with mammal watching.

We had not forgotten the Crested Tits

and eventually we were rewarded with a brief but clear view of one hanging upside-down from a pine branch in a characteristic tit-like posture, its neat little crest silhouetted against the sky. Unfortunately, no Crossbills showed up but we had done exceptionally well nevertheless.

We were now at the point where a band of lime-rich strata breaks through the generally acid soil. Almost immediately we started to come upon flowers that we had not seen all day: Wild Strawberry, Wood Sorrel, violets, speedwells and Wood Anemone. We also noticed that there were some willows

The Crested Tit (*Parus cristatus*) **is a speciality of the old Caledonian pine woods where it searches for insects at all levels in the Scots Pines. Its favourite breeding niche is the decaying stumps of dead pines which are rich both in holes and crevices to nest in and the larvae of wood-boring insects with which to feed the young.**

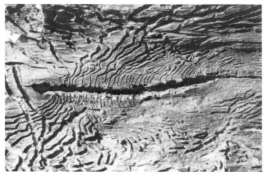

Above **Two old Scots Pines blown over by a recent gale. They will now start to play their role in the cycle of decay. Dead wood such as this might be anathema to a commercial forester but is an important element in the ecology of a natural wood.**

Above right **The galleries of a pine bark beetle. The Scots Pine, contrary to most assumptions about conifers, supports an immense variety of insect life.**

Above centre **Wood Ants** (*Formica rufa*) **moving their pupae to a safer place. How many days work must it have taken to build just one of these gigantic nests? Whatever the answer, please do not disturb them; leave them to go about their woodland ways in peace.**

growing close to the ground higher up the slope.

Sadly this part of the valley seemed to be populated almost entirely by old or decaying trees with no obvious signs of regeneration. These old age pensioners, however, were providing a marvellous habitat for the Crested Tit and a whole host of insects. Alastair set to, in an attempt to find some. We found some 'galleries' made by the pine equivalent of the Elm Bark Beetle but unfortunately because of the weather insects were generally rather scarce – that is except for the plagues of midges that were everywhere. I asked Alastair about the overall insect life of the wood.

'You can draw quite a good parallel with the oak here as, in a similar way to that tree, every aspect of the pine has its own insect exploiting the potential. There are specialist insects literally from the roots right to the tips of the branches and, of course, the cones. There are even moths which feed on the lichens that grow on the bark. There is a whole community, in fact, from pine bugs and aphids to the boring beetles associated with the dying wood.

'Some of them have become pests in the new plantations. For example, the Pine Beauty Moth has proved to be trouble not on the Scots Pine but on the Lodgepole Pine. The Forestry Commission have an experimental plot where they have Caledonian Scots Pine, "selected-out" Scots Pine, Lodgepole Pine, spruce and so on, in small squares adjacent to each other. When the Pine Beauty attacked it devastated the Lodgepole Pine, it severely attacked the "selected-out" Scots Pine but it hardly touched the Caledonian Scots Pine. If you think about it, the Caledonian pines have been their true host for the past 10 000 years and obviously some form of balance has been arrived at between the insect and its food source. I'm afraid it is the classic story of a species suddenly developing a taste for a new food source and then taking off without any constraints. The caterpillars of this moth can actually defoliate thousands of acres of the Lodgepole Pine and it is now a very serious problem.

'Another insect which is of interest, and has been actually encouraged on the continent in order to try to control caterpillars, is the Wood Ant. In most of these pine woods these Wood Ants make great nests out of needles and twigs. The ant can be a very important element in the forest because the

that would otherwise be hard to come by in these acid conditions. Butterwort, *Pinguicula vulgaris*, is widespread in Scotland and common in situations like this.'

One of the last plants that we came across was the delicate Chickweed Wintergreen, *Trientalis europaea*. It is neither a chickweed nor a wintergreen but belongs to the primrose family! This plant with its star-like flowers is only really at home in these magnificent woods and contrasts starkly with the rugged beauty of the Caledonian Scots Pines. Yet each is dependent on the successful management of the woods. We had spent a thoroughly enjoyable afternoon walking through the pass and had seen a fascinating example of our woodlands. It is only to be hoped that they will continue to be appreciated and, perhaps, eventually they will become something more than simply relics of the ancient Caledonian wood.

The Chickweed Wintergreen (*Trientalis europaea*). **A real beauty amongst the pines. It is easy to identify with its seven white petals; a member of the primrose family, despite its name.**

nests can hold hundreds of thousands of individuals, all of which are predators. These ants go off foraging, climbing up the trees and along the ground looking for insect larvae. In many woods, particularly towards the west coast but also in southern woods, these nests can be fairly thick on the ground and consequently the ants reach an almost saturation level, covering the whole woodland through all its dimensions.'

The still late afternoon air was encouraging yet more midges to come out so we started to make tracks for home. But, before we left the pass, we stopped to look at two last flowers. First, we came across a group of Butterworts which seemed to be wreaking poetic justice on the midges. Alastair explained.

'The Butterwort is an insectivorous plant. It is found characteristically on these flushed areas where you have a slight slope at the bottom of the hill. It has a flat rosette of leaves with a central flowering spike complete with a delicate blue flower. It is these leaves that are the critical part, however, as insects, such as these midges, get trapped on this slightly sticky surface. The leaves then absorb the nutrients from their bodies, supplying the plant with a source of nitrogen

Small Woods and Copses

If the last chapter left you saying, 'Oh, it's all right for those who live there, up in the wilds of the Highlands. What about me living within a sprawling suburb?' Take heart, this chapter is about shelter-belts and scraps of woodland, the like of which can be found on any urban fringe. It is also about the lifetimes' occupation of two naturalists, David Measures and his son, Simon. They visit the by-ways of their 'home patch', come rain or shine and know, through their long apprenticeship to the art, science and craft of natural history, where, how and when to look for the rich woodland life. We discovered the larvae of butterflies, the niceties of Badgers' habits and habitats and so much more on our walk with them. These things are also there to found in your own patch, so why don't you go and have a look – there is almost certainly a lot more there than you imagine.

The entrance to the home of one of Britain's favourite mammals – the Badger.

Information

Today, Britain's woodland is extremely fragmented, and while there are still a few extensive areas of woods, much of what remains are small copses or spinneys often retained in outlying areas of farmland as cover for game or as shelter-belts. These tiny patches of wood are generally not large enough to contain the complex ecosystems of plants and animals which are reliant on large areas of mature woodland but, nevertheless, they serve as important reserves for animals that have adapted to life in woodland glades or edges, and have been able to exploit the open farmland and hedgerows of today's landscape. This chapter includes a look at two different kinds of animal that live in our scattered woods. One is the Badger which, although one of Britain's best-loved mammals, is frequently overlooked, being largely a nocturnal animal. The other animals we are looking at are the butterflies, which conversely have attracted the attention of country-lovers and naturalists for centuries, with their bright colours and sun-loving habits.

Badgers

Badger of *The Wind in the Willows* is characterised as a kindly shuffling beast who keeps a tidy underground home; this is not far from the truth. Badgers are large omnivorous mammals which can reach a length of 90 centimetres (3 feet) and a weight of 16·5 kilograms (36 pounds). Their handsome black-and-white striped head and silvery-grey coat, together with the short black legs, makes them unmistakeable. They are widely distributed throughout England, Wales and most of Scotland and Ireland, although they are more local in the flat intensively cultivated regions, such as parts of East Anglia. They tend also to avoid marshy areas, preferring a mixed landscape of well-drained woods and farmland, which gives them a varied supply of food throughout the year. Badgers are most active during the summer but can be found out foraging in any month of the year. Their homes, called sets, can be very old and are often used by successive generations. They are usually dug in deep banks with dry workable soils and can be quite complex with many chambers. They have several entrances in front of which can be found great mounds of earth and bedding materials, which the Badgers use to line their chambers. They are, by and large, harmless creatures, from man's point of view, feeding on a wide range of foods from earthworms and carrion

to Bluebell bulbs and Elder berries. They have regular runs, which they use on their foraging trips and, in some forestry plantations, special gates have been erected for them, where deer and rabbit fences cross over their paths. They usually go out foraging alone but they appear to have highly developed social systems with clearly defined territories which they regularly scent mark.

The life-cycle of butterflies

The four stages of a butterfly's life-cycle are well known, these are egg, caterpillar, chrysalis, and adult butterfly or imago. Butterflies lay their eggs singly or in groups, according to the species, usually on the food plant of the caterpillar, although some species scatter their eggs in flight. The eggs, the remains of which are eaten by the newly-hatched caterpillar, are often covered with minute sculpturing. The caterpillars feed on the leaves or flowers of the host plant and are just feeding tubes, spending the day or night chewing the plant and growing larger. After they reach a certain size the skin is unable to stretch any more and splits, showing a new skin underneath which is pliable at first and stretches. The caterpillar then has space to grow, and usually moults four times in its life, becoming larger after each moult. The caterpillars are a study in themselves for, although their aim in life is to feed and grow, they are variously coloured and ornamented to camouflage and protect themselves. Many caterpillars have distasteful chemicals in the body which protect them from predators. These species are often distinctively coloured to make them easily recognized. Others are very spiny or are coloured so that they are camouflaged on their host plant. Many are covered with hairs, some of which may cause skin irritation if handled incautiously.

The length of time it takes a caterpillar to grow from first hatching to preparing for pupation varies from species to species and may take anything from two weeks to two years.

Once the caterpillar is fully grown it ceases to feed and looks for a suitable place to spend the next stage, which is the chrysalis or pupal stage. Different species have different ways of pupating to form the chrysalis, but the principle is the same for all of them. The caterpillar anchors itself firmly, then sits or hangs still. All this time a new skin is forming underneath the old one.

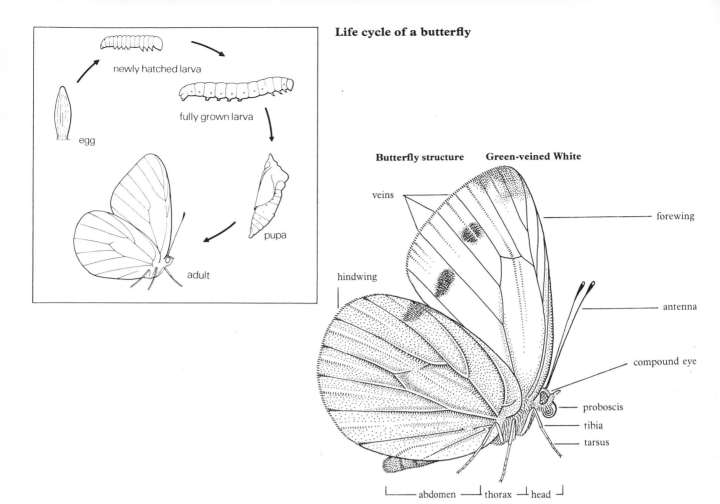

Life cycle of a butterfly

newly hatched larva

egg

fully grown larva

pupa

adult

Butterfly structure   **Green-veined White**

veins

forewing

hindwing

antenna

compound eye

proboscis

tibia

tarsus

abdomen — thorax — head

Gradually the caterpillar skin bursts revealing the soft chrysalis. Wriggling about, it eventually frees itself of the old caterpillar skin which may sometimes be found crumpled at the base of a chrysalis. The skin of the chrysalis hardens and the insect is then in an inactive stage, sometimes called the 'resting stage'. These are really misnomers because although the chrysalis itself cannot move except to wriggle, inside massive structural changes are taking place; the cells are being rearranged and special ones are multiplying to produce the adult butterfly. At a later stage some of the parts of the butterfly can be seen through the transparent skin of the chrysalis. This remarkable transformation from the crawling caterpillar to the flying butterfly is called metamorphosis.

Eventually, the chrysalis splits and does not expose a gleaming butterfly, but a bedraggled insect with crumpled wings. This hangs motionless for a time while the wings expand and dry and it is some time before the insect is strong enough to flap its wings and take flight. The males often emerge before the females, which makes it more likely that every emerging female will be

mated. They recognize each other by colour, pattern, and certain scents or pheromones.

After this stage there is no more growth; small butterflies do not grow into larger ones. The butterfly with its wings expanded and dry, moves off to feed, find a mate, and start the life-cycle again.

The adult butterfly may live for a few weeks, six months or more. The whole life-cycle may take place in one or two months or may take more than a year. When the life-cycle is relatively short there may be several generations (broods) in one year. If the adult butterfly hibernates over the winter it will come out in spring to lay its eggs, perhaps during April and May. The adult usually dies after egg laying and so there will only be eggs and some adults in the field. Later, there will probably only be caterpillars, as the adults that over-wintered will have died. These caterpillars, once fully grown, will pupate and then hatch to produce a new generation of butterflies in June and July. Some species have overlapping broods and there may be all stages in the field during the summer months.

(Extract from *Hamlyn Nature Guides : Butterflies* by Paul Whalley)

Small Woods and Copses

with
David Measures

On a warm July day we went up to Nottinghamshire to meet the artist-naturalist David Measures and his son, Simon. We had come to walk around some of their local woodland and look at the wildlife, notably the butterflies, which David had portrayed so marvellously in his book, *Bright Wings of Summer*, and also some of the mammals, which so often go unnoticed in our countryside. The day turned out to be an object lesson in how, if you make a close study of your own 'home patch', you can discover enough to probably keep you interested for a life-time. Every hedgerow, every glade and bank had its own little story, which over the years David and Simon had pieced together to provide a fascinating natural and man-made history of their own quiet stretch of the English countryside. I am quite sure that if I had not been with them I would have probably walked around the woods and footpaths and only seen a hundredth of the wildlife that they were able to show me.

On our way up to the main wooded area near David's village our route took us beside a large field which at one time had been part of the old manorial 'open field' system and still showed signs of the traditional ridge and furrow pattern. Each villager would work a few strips scattered across the field so that everyone had a share of both the fertile and the poor land. This system worked successfully for many centuries whilst farming was essentially carried out at a subsistence level. The enclosure movements of the Seventeenth and Eighteenth Centuries did away with most of these open fields as farming became increasingly commercial and profitable and, today, there are very few left. A notable example, however, was not far away at Laxton in Nottinghamshire.

The lane up to this ancient field was called Woodhouse Lane, which indicated that it was a main route to and from the area of woodland for, as well as providing the cut timbers for the construction of local buildings, the villagers were allowed to collect firewood and fencing. So we set about following the stream bank at the base of the 'Great West Field' up to an area beyond that had provided woodland grazing for the villagers' livestock, again under the old manorial system. Before we reached this, however, Simon was very keen to show us the home of one of our best loved native mammals – the Badger.

On a clay bank on the opposite side of the ditch from the footpath were some tell-tale holes which were just visible under some Elder trees and behind some clumps of Stinging Nettles. Although they knew the set was there, David and Simon were not sure if it was currently occupied. Simon scuttled down the bank and across the ditch to have a look. It was not long before his obvious enthusiasm drew us all over. Under the trees were the unmistakable signs of Badgers. David looked over the area around the entrances to the set and immediately confirmed that it was in use.

'Marvellous, I see what Simon means, this is very active.' The main indication of this was a couple of small pits with droppings in them. These were Badger latrines. In one pit the dung was visibly darker and more oily.

'How many animals have deposited here?' I asked.

The strange deformation of the bark on this elm tree is the result of years of browsing by horses along the side of the 'Great West Field'. Although the fence has prevented them from completely killing off the tree, their repeated attempts to reach the bark have permanently marked it.

'This would have been left last night by two Badgers before leaving to go off for a night's foraging. Some of it is drier and is probably two or three days' old. As they are large droppings they will have been deposited by adults.' Simon pointed out that there were a lot of barley grains in them.

'The trace is chiefly grain, which they enjoy at this time of year, but they probably contain other remains that are harder to pick out. The wing cases of beetles, which are fairly indigestible, are another food remain that can be prominent in Badger droppings. I asked David what their main diet would be?

'They are great scavengers and will eat almost anything: grain at this time of year, dead mammals, worms are a great favourite, as they are with Foxes, and it is the worms, perhaps, that cause the dark oily appearance of some of the dung. They are basically foraging creatures and will travel miles each night in search of food. I can remember when I was Simon's age, I found a dead sow Badger by the roadside, and when I cut its stomach open I found about twenty frogs inside. All of them were whole and I half expected them to hop out in the fashion of Jonah and the Whale! Badgers will also dig out the nests of rabbits and mice in the stubble. You can sometimes find bees' and, more frequently, wasps' nests that they have dug up, with discarded chunks of empty broodcomb lying by the great scrapes of the Badger.' Simon then discovered some more latrines down the slope, confirming further that this site was in regular use.

Moving on and a short distance away from the main latrines, was a large hole with a pile of grass and straw at its entrance. Simon moved across to have a closer look.

'The grass goes right down into the hole. This is probably the main entrance to the system at the moment.' The dry grass was fresh bedding, which is one of the chief signs of an occupied Badger set. Badgers appear to be meticulous about their hygiene and will change the old bedding at intervals for fresh material, which they drag down into the chambers deep underground. While we were by the entrance David and Simon recounted some of the highlights of their local Badger watching.

'I'd always been led to believe that when you went out Badger watching you needed to take the greatest care and that people who

Above left **The entrance to the Badger set by the footpath.**

Above **Two Badgers rooting around in the woodland floor.**

Below **Badger droppings in a freshly scraped latrine. Note the undigested grains of barley.**

Badgers are great opportunists and will eat almost anything. Here a Badger has scraped away the earth around a wasps' nest to get at the larvae. Note the scratch marks on the root in the foreground.

Simon peering into the entrance of the Badger set. Beside him is a large mound of bedding straw.

ones that night were the ones that seemed unafraid and they kept coming up to the fence where we were standing, to investigate what we were. The adults would then blunder out from the shelter of the thorn cover, grab the cubs by the scruff of the neck and pull them back again.

'We had found some trees that provided a good place to watch the Badgers from and on another evening, just as we were about to climb a tree, we suddenly realised that at our feet there was a small cub, just standing there staring at us. Unfortunately we didn't take too much notice, as we expected to see plenty more once we were settled in the tree. But apart from an adult that came ambling past, it was the only one we saw all evening.'

A tree nearby the set had some scratch marks on the bark and I asked David whether these had been made by Badgers.

'Yes, but it is not what is known as a scratching tree, where they clean their claws – later on we will have a look at an old willow which shows that – but this is the result of them scraping around looking for grubs. Beetle larvae, that they find in rotting wood, are a particularly important source of protein during the hard winter months.

'Whilst we are down here on this bank it is worth recalling that had we walked this way last year, we would have found something very different as then, at these holes, there was a rather obvious litter of dead animals – half-eaten rabbits and even the remains of dead chickens. These were the untidy signs of a vixen that was using this system for her earth. There is often this interchange between Foxes and Badgers in the use of a set and it is interesting that both of these animals will use such sunny banks. In fact, I am sure Foxes prefer a warm situation although it is conspicuous to every passer-by. Both animals need these deep banks to avoid flooding and also this red marl is easy to excavate. There is a set on a ten metre bank near here riddled with holes all the way up and down, with great mounds of cast bedding and earth in front of the entrances, creating quite a sculptural feel, like an old cave system.

'Whilst we are talking about the Badger I should mention the current controversy: the role that the Badger takes in spreading Bovine Tuberculosis. Around here I would say that it is very, very seldom, that cattle are going to be able to 'nose' against a piece of Badger dung, which is how they could

weren't able to keep still for long periods, would find it almost impossible to be successful.' Simon took up the story.

'The first time we tried to watch some Badgers we went out during the day and found a corner of a field where all the grass had been flattened at the top of a set. We then went back in the evening before it was dusk and to our amazement as we approached we found about ten to twelve Badgers already running around, shuffling and squeaking.' David continued.

'They were thundering around. It was a bit like a circus ring which we would hardly have dared put a foot into, as they appeared quite formidable when they were charging. They are large heavy beasts. The young pick up the disease. This is because, as we have seen here, they always use hedgebanks, the corners of woods, or go just inside the edges of the woods to make their latrines. We can show you latrine after latrine, which we have been plotting over the years, and I would say that, certainly in this part of the Midlands, where thorn, Elder and other trees abound, you never get a Badger depositing out in open pasture. Unfortunately, I can't say the same of somewhere like Derbyshire, where in the hard limestone districts, the Badger probably goes down to the stream banks to scrape in earth which might then mean that a cow could come within the vicinity of the dung. But even there it must be remembered that frequently, the following evening, in digging a fresh pit they will cover up the previous evening's dung. In any case there is no evidence of T.B. in Badgers in the Midland Counties.'

As we were talking Simon had been searching around for some more signs and had found a Badger's hair. It had a distinct pattern of black at the tip, then white in the middle and black again at the base. It was very stiff and until recently these Badger hairs were widely used as shaving brushes. A good place to find the hairs is on barbed wire or on a low thorn bush that overhangs a regular Badger run.

Before we moved on David pointed out some small black caterpillars in a clump of Stinging Nettles nearby. These were Peacock Butterfly larvae, most of which were beneath a web-like 'tent'. The caterpillars were a glossy black colour with tufts of black hairs and minute white spots. They were very small compared with a fully grown caterpillar and still had some greeny-grey about them so were probably in their second instar or skin-shedding phase. A Peacock caterpillar goes through four of these before it pupates. I asked David about the 'tent'. Was it some sort of safety device?

'Yes, it can be used in a way like a safety net. It also gives them some anchorage against the buffeting of the wind or worse still, the pouring rain. They will also take refuge within it during the cold of the night. Interestingly, it is not entirely coincidence that the caterpillars are here, as there is a link between the Badgers and the Peacock Butterflies. This bank has some nice warm areas which have been regularly trampled and consequently the earth has been exposed. The butterflies will settle on these sunny

Above **The caterpillars of the Peacock Butterfly on a Stinging Nettle. The web-like structure covering the plant provides them with both anchorage and protection.**

Left **The hairs of a Badger caught on a low strand of barbed wire over one of their regular pathways.**

"hot spots" with their wings open to soak up the sun. Being "cold-blooded" this gives them the boost they need to fly around looking for food and take part in their territorial and courtship flights. Also the Peacock loves to feed on the juices in the Badger droppings. If you watch them at the edge of a wood you might be lucky enough to spot them leaving the sun and disappearing into the dappled shade to feed off a Badger dropping.

'The Peacock together with the Small Tortoiseshell and the Brimstone butterflies are the longest lived of the British butterflies, as they all hibernate. They can live up to eight months and the Brimstone, which we will look at later, can go up to a year. So

Above **The sole surviving Wild Service Tree with a Hawthorn at its base. This tree was once part of the natural woodland cover and now stands almost alone in a field of barley.**

Right **The shelter belt at the top of the ridge. This small area of woodland was planted after the enclosure of the land and now provides a home for a wide variety of woodland animals.**

marked the western edge of the original open field. It has been found that as a rough guide you can age a hedge by counting the number of species of tree present over a short stretch. As a general rule, one new species colonises a hedge every one hundred years. So a hedgerow with seven or eight species occurring within any 30 metres of its length, as with the hedge here, could be seven or eight hundred years old, which would coincide with the age of the medieval field system. David pointed out some of the species: Hawthorn, Hazel, Oak, Ash, Elder, Sloe, Elm, Field Maple and the occasional glistening Holly. This method of dating hedges is used quite widely but it can be misleading, so it is best used in conjunction with early maps of the area. On the other side of the hedge was another field with a crop of golden barley, but it has not always been like that as David explained.

'This hedge was the old boundary between the arable fields and what was likely to have been "woodland grazing". This would have looked like an open wood with scrubby trees, where the villagers would have brought their pigs and various livestock to feed. There are indications in the existing hedges of the original wooded nature of the area. For example, there are some immense Hazels, Crab Apple and Maple boles in some of the stretches and further over in one field is a sole surviving Wild Service Tree. This tree is more common in the south, particularly in Kent where its distinctive bark gives it the name Chequers Tree, but up here in the Midlands it is very local. We have combed the area pretty thoroughly and the only places that you find them now are in the parish boundaries that coincide with the natural boundaries of the old stream banks. The Wild Service Tree seeds itself infrequently and takes a long while to become established so that in these parts it indicates primary woodland. The specimen we have on this land is standing on its own in a field as the hedgerow that it was in was grubbed-up, but luckily an old farmer pointed out that it was the only tree of its sort on the owner's land and they left it. So at one time it would have been in woodland, then when most of that was cleared it survived as an important hedgerow tree and now there it stands as a final relict, a little island in a field of barley.'

Whilst we continued our walk up to the ridge where most of the remaining woodland was situated, David talked about the

they have to be knowing and able creatures in order to survive bird predators and all the harsh weather conditions, as well as exploit a wide range of food sources as the seasons change. Some butterflies are short-lived, darting, fierce creatures, such as the Small Copper, but these long-lived ones tend to be more sedate. They go into hiding and reappear according to the warmth of the sun.'

Taking care not to knock the caterpillars from their leaves, we clambered back on to the path. About twenty metres further on we arrived at a great thick hedge which skills and enjoyment of being a naturalist.

'To really find out what is happening in a woodland or wherever, you need to visit it regularly and walk quietly. Often the best approach is find a well-protected spot with clear views and let the animals come to you rather than trying to give chase to them. The walking part of a day out, as enjoyable as it is, is not the best way to study the country-side. It should really be a means to an end, for it is at those times when you remain in one place that you start to see things. I remember once I was out near here with my dog and we saw a vixen crossing a field. I was leaning against a maple but my dog, a big labrador, gave chase and the vixen headed off towards the wood and as she did this she looked back at the dog. It was almost as if she was laughing at this great heavy creature lumbering after her. In a short time she lost him in the wood and then, when she thought she was safe, she trotted back across the field and went right past the tree I was still leaning against!

'I think this business of getting to know the habits of creatures, being able to stalk them and predict their whereabouts is a throw back to our primitive origins. Today, whether you are out studying the habits of a mammal, bird or insect, out with a gun, a camera, or a notebook it stems from the importance of being able to identify and locate things, which in the past was strongly tied up with survival. Those that had developed this skill were the ones, in a sense, that could be the most adaptable during a crisis. Today the enjoyment and urge to acquire a similar knowledge about a piece of land or neighbourhood, and to know which plants or animals are of benefit is still latent. But this is a skill which takes a long while, indeed, a life-time's study, in which to be proficient. So there's plenty of time for us Simon, isn't there?'

We had now arrived at the highest stretch of land. I asked David about the origins of the present landscape.

'This was referred to as the "moor", but not in the sense of moorland covered with heather, rather as simply an unclaimed high area, most likely wooded and later used as scrub grazing. It was cleared and hedged during the enclosure movements, around 1770. However, they seemed to have cleared the area too well and had to replant the crest of the moor with elms, which acted as a shelter belt. Most of the woodland here is derived from this period.

The distinctive fruits of the Spindle Tree. These will open later in the year to expose the bright orange covering of the seed. These colourful fruits are attractive to birds which help spread the seeds.

The heavily sculptured bole of an old willow. But there is more to it than appears at first glance, for the soft wood on the hollow inside of the tree has been scratched by the claws of many Badgers.

'This, as with many other local woods in the Midlands, is comprised largely of elms, and the present worry is that they are being attacked by the Dutch Elm Disease, which will soon devastate them. A large number of the hedgerow trees have already been affected and many have already been felled. Ironically, the dying elm provides a mar-vellous, transient habitat for wood-boring beetles and also the woodpeckers that are seeking them. The Lesser Spotted Wood-pecker is now appearing around here for the first time, whereas previously, it has been

An all too familiar sight in our hedgerows. Dead elms struck down in their prime by Dutch Elm Disease. In order that our landscape does not become permanently denuded of trees it is vital that new trees are planted to replace these. It is also important that the existing hedgerows are maintained in such a way that young saplings are able to establish themselves. Unfortunately modern farming practice with its flail mowers often prevents this. However, with a little thought these trees can be cut around and so allowed to thrive.

confined to local pockets in the southern Midlands. Another benefit resulting from the dying elms occurred during that hot summer of 1976, when wild flowers were few and far between, which meant that butterflies and other nectar feeding insects were having a hard time. Sap was pouring forth from the holes created by the beetles in the elm bark, presumably caused by the excessive heat. There were places where we came across puddles of this sap at which butterflies, bees, hornets and wasps were all busily feeding. Here we found Red Admirals and honey bees feeding at the holes in live elms. This habit of the Red Admiral has been recorded on the continent but, as far as I am aware, has never before been noted as occurring in Britain.

'There has always been this great tradition of collecting butterflies in this country and yet remarkably little study has been made of their habits in the wild state. It astounds me how many people are still trained to capture butterflies with a net and not shown how to observe them in the field by watching, taking notes and photographs. It is easier to photograph butterflies than people imagine. It is simply a question of stealth – being able to move up on the creature so gradually that it hardly notices you – perhaps this is easier for Simon, here, with his supple limbs than the older generation with their creaking knees!'

We were now in the cool of the woodland and David and Simon were looking for Badger tracks on the muddy path. There were plenty of dog tracks with their great pads but before long, they had found a little

gully where a badger had ambled across leaving its distinctive marks. Just to make the picture complete a Fox had also walked nearby. Simon pointed out the key features which distinguished them.

'That's a Badger print, as you can see all four main toe pads are in a line at the front, unlike the Fox print which has its pads close together, two in front and two behind. With a domestic dog the toe pads are usually splayed out!' David added that when you have learnt the main characteristics, the telling part is being able to distinguish between a young Badger and an older one, or between a Fox cub and a vixen and also, a big old dog Fox, which can look similar to a domestic dog.

We wandered on through the wood, which consisted mostly of Ash and elms, with the occasional oak. Along one side of the wood was an older coppiced section. This was still providing fencing posts for the farmer. There was a more varied mixture of trees here with Guelder Rose and Hazel stools growing amongst the larger trees. Some old Holly trees were growing around the fringe of the coppice. Beside one of these David pointed out a small tree.

'This tree is unusual in this area. It is a Spindle and, apart from indicating that we are on a limey soil, it also tells us that this part of the wood has probably been here for a long while. The Spindle is very slow growing, seldom being more than five metres in height, with this characteristic narrow stem. The wood from this tree was traditionally used for spindles, hence the name, and furthermore the word "spinster" was derived from spindle as it was reckoned that a spinster had more time to spin than a wife with children. They have these gorgeous pink and orange fruits in the autumn, which the birds feed on and it is quite possible that a bird would have brought the seed in to this coppice which started this tree.'

We then made our way out along the edge of the wood for a while. Some crows were calling noisily above us, circling between the topmost branches of the trees. David and Simon were very aware of them, as the crows had a special place in their journeys to this woodland. David pointed up at them and as they wheeled above us he explained.

'Those crows are the watch-dogs; they are the most intelligent birds of the woodland. Unfortunately they are now our biggest curse because of something we did a couple of years ago. They have never for-

A woodland ride providing a succession of micro-habitats from closely cropped grass in the centre through taller grasses and brambles to the lower branches of the smaller trees and shrubs. Butterflies, in particular, like to feed and sun themselves in these linear 'glades'.

Idealised tracks of three of our larger mammals that might be encountered on a woodland walk. (A) Badger, with its broad hind pad and parallel row of toe pads; (B) Fox, with its closely spaced pads, notice the hair traces between the toes; (C) Domestic dog with its three-lobed hind pad and splayed toe pads (After Lawrence and Brown, 1967).

gotten it or forgiven us since then. They seem to recognise us from all the other passers-by that journey along this footpath.' Simon told us what had happened.

'We found a Maple tree with a crow's nest which was fairly easy to climb up to. We would visit the nest every few days to watch the eggs hatch out and the chicks develop. Sometimes while we were standing swaying in the wind at the edge of the nest, making sketches and paintings of the chicks, the parents would return and dive bomb us. At that height it was quite frightening. Even after their young had flown they persistently hounded us, even finding us at dusk.'

We had now come to a steep bank outside the wood where some old willows were growing. One, in particular, was the biggest willow I had ever seen. Its base must have been over seven metres (24 feet) in circumference but what we had come to look at was actually inside the tree. One part of it was hollow, probably where a branch had fallen off many years ago and, inside this, the wood was scored with the scratch marks of many Badgers that had climbed up inside the tree and scraped their claws clean on the soft inner wood and no doubt sampled any wood-boring grubs they uncovered.

The willow was at the corner of a small meadow that was hedged in by some very old trees. David showed us a Field Maple that was perhaps 350 years old, an old Crab Apple, and some large Hazels that were twined around a Hawthorn. All this was a clear indication that this area had at some stage been covered with old woodland.

Further down the bank David pointed out

another Badger set. This one was more secluded than the one we had seen earlier, being surrounded by tall elms and with a covering of Elder trees. These Elders were probably there as a result of the Badgers, as they, like Foxes, enjoy feasting on the Elder berries, the seeds of which are then deposited in the Badger latrines along with their own supply of fertilizer – the Badger dung. So it is a common feature throughout Britain to find Elder trees associated with Badger sets. David pointed out that also these sets can be many centuries old, although not necessarily in continuous occupation for that length of time.

From there we crossed back over to the main woods. The area that we had now arrived at was owned by the Forestry Commission. When David first started visiting the woods seventeen years ago, it was still mostly old deciduous woodland in the process of being felled. Since then they have been selectively replacing the traditional wood with conifers. So for David the interest has been largely in studying the way that the clearance and regeneration of trees, as well as the planting, has affected the wildlife.

'It has been a marvellously successful mix so far. Over there you can see we have an oak tree next to a Lawson's Cypress which, in turn, is partly blocked from view by a Hazel. The cutting down of the old trees and the creation of these wide rides in the wood has meant that there has been an increase in the overall open space within the wood and this has benefited the ground flora which in turn has meant that there has been a large increase in the variety of insects.

Below **Brimstone feeding on knapweed. This is one of the first butterflies to be seen in spring. Its butter-yellow colour is perhaps the origin of the name 'butterfly'.**

Bottom **A newly emerged Small Skipper. The males emerge first to set up their territories and can easily be distinguished by the dark line of scent scales on their forewings.**

'Of the British woodland butterflies, we have none of the rarities and do not even have the Speckled Wood up here in the Midlands, so we have to concentrate on the other common woodland species – the Brimstone. If we go further along this ride hopefully we should find some caterpillars of the Brimstone.' As we walked along the ride we talked about the life history of this remarkable insect.

'Brimstones are usually the first butterflies that you see in the year and it is on those first sunny days that they will begin courtship. With luck you will sometimes find the male and female paired, hanging on to the underside of a Bramble leaf. Their silvery-lemon undersides can be so conspicuous that other males are attracted down to hover around trying to join in with the mating. This causes the established male to flutter and so to flick them off. It is one of the earliest butterflies to lay eggs. You can find them even before their host plants, the buckthorns, have come into full leaf, providing there are leaf buds. On the first warm day after the female has been mated, she will start depositing her eggs. These are cemented at right angles to the undersides of the scaly buds so, as the leaves begin to open, the eggs travel with them. About this time the

first spring warblers, the Chiff-chaffs and Willow Warblers, come along and as soon as the eggs hatch and the larvae are large enough to be eaten, the warblers are there seeking them out.

'The Brimstone is essentially a woodland butterfly, but you will often notice it travelling alongside roads and hedges. The reason for this is that, in the absence of woodland, the only place the butterflies are likely to find their host plant is in the hedgerows, some of which might be a relic of the original wood. There are just two species of tree that they are looking for, one is the Common or Purging Buckthorn and the other is the Alder Buckthorn. These are not very conspicuous trees and, if you are not a botanist, it is almost easier to let the butterfly lead you to one. In fact, I discovered the Alder Buckthorn along here because I had been following a female Brimstone. There are lots of the Common Buckthorn around but I had been looking for five or six years for an Alder Buckthorn before this butterfly showed me the way. It is a tree that prefers damp conditions, provided here by a ditch running along the side of the ride. Incidentally, the Alder Buckthorn was extensively sought during the war years, as it was found that its wood, which has a very uniform cell structure, made very reliable charcoal fuses for ammunition.

'Here it is. Its leaves have smooth edges unlike those of the Common Buckthorn which are finely toothed. When I was along here a fortnight ago, there were quite a few caterpillars but once the warblers have discovered that there are caterpillars on a tree they will repeatedly search for them. You can see where the leaves have been eaten by the caterpillars but for the moment I can't see one. The female would probably have laid in the region of forty-five eggs at all levels up and down the tree, but you will need as sharp an eye as the warbler's to spot one. . . . It is interesting to reflect that to maintain its population – and the Brimstone does seem to keep a fairly stable one – only two out of every hundred larvae need to survive. So, perhaps we should not be too dismayed at the birds' good fortune here. . . . Ah! There's one right at the base of the tree on that low branch. Look how it has attached itself to the base of the leaf and is lying along the mid-rib; that is very characteristic. Also see how it "flicks" its body when I put my finger close to it; almost like a snake. That is a defensive mechanism to alarm a bird – a juvenile, perhaps, before it has acquired the taste – but looking at the rest of the tree it is apparent that it doesn't always work. The caterpillar is a green colour and blends exactly with the shade of the leaf and this one is fairly large and it won't be long before it pupates. When it emerges as a new butterfly in August, if nothing befalls it, it will live right through to next summer.

'The adult butterfly throughout its life favours the sanctuary of blackberry bushes and will often hibernate in a suitable bush. Some of them go into the thickets before blackberrying time so people crashing about in search of the berries are sometimes unwittingly in the vicinity of the Brimstone's wintering quarters.

'They can withstand the sharpest frosts of winter. I understand that it was from the hibernating Brimstone that the chemistry of antifreeze was discovered. To think, the conversion from nectar to protein, and then to the antifreeze we use today in our motor cars has come from the study of a butterfly. So butterflies have their uses even to our present technological civilisation!

'Other British butterflies that regularly hibernate, are the Peacock and the Small Tortoiseshell, both are common and can be found hibernating in lofts, garden sheds and out-houses. A fourth hibernating butterfly, the Comma, is more usually found in the southern half of Britain, although there are records of it in this area many years ago.

The caterpillar of the Brimstone on a leaf of one of its host plants, Alder Buckthorn. The position it has taken up along the mid-rib of the leaf is characteristic of this species.

The caterpillars of the Small Tortoiseshell on Stinging Nettles. Nettles are an important host plant for many butterflies including the Red Admiral, Peacock and Comma, as well as the Small Tortoiseshell.

'In spite of the glorious sun there are few butterflies to be seen. There is usually a lull in July and this has been particularly noticeable this year. In August the progeny of the common species will be emerging as the first or second brood of the season, but if I take you along the open ride, through the youngest plantation, there are lush grasses, red clover and trefoils in flower on which Small Skippers flourish. They will be emerging today if we are lucky, brought forth by the day's sunshine.'

So we then moved on leaving the Brimstone caterpillar in peace. Sure enough further along in a more open part of the plantation we came across some newly emerged Small Skippers, magnificent in their glowing orange, perfect in every detail. It was interesting to see that they were all males with the distinctive black stripe on their angled forewing. Females emerge a day or two after to allow the males time to take up the best perches and to get to know their territory.

We finished our walk along the edge of the wood, where the farmer had dumped some large piles of farmyard manure. Here there were some caterpillars in amongst the verge nettles. David described them.

'These are the larvae of the Small Tortoiseshell and interestingly, the reason that there are so many here, and I have previously counted eleven different groups along this one stretch, is a result of the proximity of the manure heaps! The adults are attracted by the warmth generated in the manure and the

many facets of the stack, giving an ample selection of ideal perches to sun in, no matter what time of day. Mated, the females then come over to this growth of nettles, their host plant, to lay their eggs. If we look closely we can see that although they look similar to the Peacock caterpillars, which we also found on nettles earlier on, these have distinct narrow yellow lines along the body. Again, like the Peacock, they are gregarious and these are living in and around web-like "tents". Here you can see that the larger ones are "flicking" like the Brimstone caterpillar. These larvae must be unpleasant tasting for I know of only the cuckoo that will feed on them – hence the large numbers of Tortoiseshells we see.

'The pleasure of being out for the best part of the day has given us the chance to notice how a variety of these common creatures fare. It is always satisfying in mid-season to reassess that age-long, yet increasingly critical, relationship that exists between the farmers, their crops, the more permanent hedgerows and treebelts and their associated wildlife.'

We left the caterpillars nervously twitching in amongst the nettles and headed back for home. It had been an exciting day, we had seen many different things and yet it had not been a mere question of listing species or blandly recording numbers. David and Simon were looking at the animals and plants as part of the overall community and relating the various elements not only to the present landscape but also to the past history of their small part of the British countryside. It had been a real privilege to have spent a day out in the field with them and I can tell you that as soon as I arrived back home I went out and looked at my local wood with new eyes.

A Speckled Wood sunning itself in a woodland glade. This woodland butterfly is common over much of southern England but is much more local over the rest of Britain.

An Oak Wood in Summer

The oak, be it Pedunculate or Sessile or even some intermediate between the two, is the stout heart of the British woodlands. It has so many places in our history, and fortunately is still not uncommon in our landscapes either as a dominant or co-dominant tree in mixed woodland, as standards in old coppice, or as single trees in farmland. I say 'fortunately', because of all our trees, the oak provides both food and a home for the greatest variety of insects and other invertebrates. Likewise, its rough fissured bark offers safe anchorage for an immense range of epiphytic lichens.

David Streeter is a natural historian par excellence, *a teacher in the grandest manner and a stalwart of nature conservation and especially of the Sussex Trust for Nature Conservation.*

Put the two together, Quercus *and Streeter, in the Sussex scene and you have got hours of fascination.*

A Wealden oak wood in high summer.

Information

The most important of our native broad-leaved woodland trees are Pedunculate Oak, Sessile Oak, Elm, Ash and Beech. By far and away the most typical of these are the two oaks, which are discussed in detail in the walk. The main factors influencing which type of wood predominates are the climate, soil and the influence of man.

An interesting example is the distribution of Beech in Britain. It appears that Beech woods are at the northern edge of their range in our islands, and probably only naturally occur in southern England and some parts of Wales. They are further restricted by the fact that they grow best on well-drained soils, such as the chalk downs of the south-east. However, this picture has been substantially altered by man. Beech is valuable as a timber in furniture making and was extensively planted in central England to supply the needs of this industry. Its ability to grow on the thin soils of chalk escarpments meant that it was also frequently planted to provide shelter belts. In recent centuries, it has also been widely planted for landscape and amenity purposes. Therefore, today, it is possible to find stands of this splendid tree growing almost anywhere in Britain, although it is still noticeably commoner in the south. Where it does grow, it casts a dense shade and in the south some interesting plants particularly adapted to surviving under their cover can be found. These include the Bird's Nest Orchid, *Neottia nidus-avis,* which is a saprophyte feeding on humus through the agency of a fungus.

Ash woods are another interesting example. In areas of the south of England they tend to form a 'nurse' crop for Beech and oaks, but in other areas, such as the calcareous soils in the north and west, they appear to form the climax woodland. Unlike the Beech, they create a fairly open canopy and consequently the ground flora can be very rich. Some of these Ash woods appear to be of recent origin and have probably arisen on cleared sites. Pollen analysis has shown that the original climax woodland would probably have consisted mainly of Wych Elm or Small-leaved Lime, which today are far rarer as woodland trees. Where woods exist on craggy escarpments which might not have been cleared as, for example, in some areas of the Peak District and the Mendips, they are very species rich, with whitebeams and a varied ground flora, including plants such as hellebores and bellflowers.

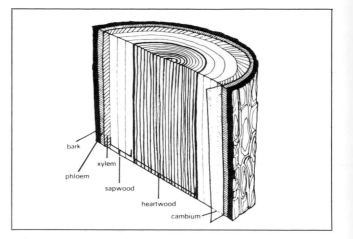

The structure of a tree
Stem and wood structure

The thickened main stem of a tree is the trunk; that part below the lowest branches is called the bole.

A transverse section or slice across a mature trunk will reveal three obvious layers; the inner heartwood, or xylem, the outer layer of corky bark, and a middle layer, the bast, or phloem. The xylem forms the main part of the thickened stem and can be seen to be composed of two parts; a central, dark coloured heartwood that contains no sap, and an outer, lighter coloured sapwood that if filled with water and dissolved substances passing from the soil. The heartwood, in other words, is dead and has ceased to function. With time it gradually fills with the hard, durable thickening material called lignin, the substance we call wood. Surrounding the wood cylinder is the phloem, through which pass the food products manufactured in the leaves. Outside the phloem is another layer, the cork layer, which varies in thickness according to the species of the tree. Bark and cork are both protective dead tissues.

Gymnosperm heartwood is called softwood and is made up of only two types of cells. The main conductive elements, called tracheids, are long, thickened fibres running end to end in the wood. The other cells, called parenchyma, consist of thin-walled brick-shaped cells arranged in radiating rows, known as medullary rays, and it is these which give the characteristic grain to finished timbers.

Angiosperm heartwood is called hardwood and differs from gymnosperm wood in that it consists of three, rather than two, types of cells. Instead of having the fibrous support and the conducting tissues functionally combined into a tracheid, hardwoods have separate large hollow, rather thin-walled conductive cells, called vessels, and rather more solid, thick-walled, sharp-pointed supportive cells, called fibres. The parenchyma are arranged in medullary rays in much the same way as gymnosperm wood.

Leaves

The leaves are the food factories of plants. They are specialized organs, which utilize water and dissolved minerals passed up by the roots and the stems from the soil, and carbon dioxide absorbed from the atmosphere through the stomata on the leaf surface, to manufacture complex food substances. They do this in the green part of the leaves, the chlorophyll, using sunlight as the energy source. The complex food substances, particularly carbohydrates, are redistributed around other organs of the plant by the phloem.

A typical leaf is composed of a leaf-stalk or petiole which attaches to the stem, and a blade (lamina) which is the functional part. In some cases the blade can be borne directly on the stem (in which case it is said to be sessile).

The leaf-blade is provided with a network of veins and the whole arrangement is called the venation pattern. The veins consist of xylem and phloem tissue, catering respectively for the transport of water and minerals into the leaf and the manufactured food substances out of the leaf. In some leaves there is one main vein which branches irregularly and further subdivides in a reticulate pattern – this is called net venation. Such a pattern is characteristic of elm, oak and maple leaves. In other species, particularly the monocotyledonous trees (the palms, etc.) and conifers, instead of one main vein with branches there are several veins of equal size running parallel to each other, a pattern called parallel venation.

(Extract from *The Hamlyn Guide to Trees of Britain and Europe* by C. J. Humphries)

The following is a selection of some interesting areas of broad-leaved woodland around Britain. It is suggested that if you are intending to visit any of these woods that you consult some of the many regional guides for further information regarding access. See also the woodlands listed on page

Loch Lomond, Strathclyde. National Nature Reserve. Woodland dominated by Sessile Oak. Inchcailloch, an island in Loch Lomond, is a particularly fine example of native woodland.

Borrowdale Woods, Cumbria. National Trust. Excellent Sessile Oakwoods amidst dramatic lakeland scenery. Good mosses and lichens. Nature trails.

Sherwood Forest, Nottinghamshire. Country Park. A surviving relict of the once extensive forest still remains near Edwinstowe. Mostly Pedunculate and Sessile Oaks including the celebrated Major Oak.

Cannock Chase, Staffordshire. Country Park. Varied scenery including heathland, grassland and woodland including oak and birch wood; once a royal hunting forest.

Charnwood Forest, Leicestershire. Fragmented remains of once extensive forest can be seen at Bradgate Park and Swithland Woods Country Park. Includes interesting rock outcrops and ruins, also herds of deer.

Epping Forest, Essex. Large area of ancient forest with public access (see page 110). Pollarded Beech and Hornbeam sections as well as interesting oak and birch woods. Excellent for autumn fungi. Hatfield, Hainault and Norsey Woods in Essex are also worth visiting.

Burnham Beeches, Buckinghamshire. Country Park. Very good Beech wood including pollarded specimens with Pedunculate Oaks and birches. Nature Trails. Good for autumn fungi.

Windsor Forest, Berkshire. Mixed woodland including conifer plantations and ornamental gardens, but also some interesting natural woodland. Good birdwatching and worth a visit for the autumn fungi.

Box Hill, Surrey. National Trust. Famous chalk hill with fine Beech woods and stands of Box. Juniper Hall Field Centre close-by runs many courses through the year.

Scords Wood, Kent. Partly National Trust. Interesting area with wide variety of tree species including Beech, Pedunculate and Sessile Oak and Ash.

Savernake Forest, Wiltshire. Forestry Commission woodland. Some areas are ancient broad-leaved forest which are of great entomological and botanical interest. Red, Fallow and Roe deer are present. Nature Trails.

New Forest, Hampshire/Dorset. Extensive area managed by the Forestry Commission with good public access. Wide variety of woodland types from mature Beech and oak woods to birch woods and pine plantations.

Brownsea Island, Dorset. National Trust, reserve managed by Dorset Naturalists' Trust. Island in Poole Harbour with oak woods. One of the few places in England still with Red Squirrels.

Forest of Dean, Herefordshire. Forestry Commission woodland. Extensive area of ancient woodland with modern conifer plantations. Worth visiting Symonds Yat. Nature Trails.

Wyre Forest, Herefordshire/Worcestershire. Partly Forestry Commission managed area of ancient woodland. Includes excellent Sessile Oak woods on acid soils.

Maentwrog, Gwynedd. Natural Nature Reserve. Area in Vale of Ffestiniog open during summer. Predominately Sessile Oak woods. Nature Trails. Study Centre.

Correl Glen Forest, Fermanagh. Forest Nature Reserve. Mixed deciduous woodland. Nature Trails.

Burren, Clare. Extraordinary area of hazel scrub on limestone. Interesting ground flora. Good for ferns, lichens and mosses.

Killarney Oakwoods, Kerry. Sessile Oak woods with well-developed understorey. Good for ferns, lichens and mosses.

An Oak Wood in Summer
with
David Streeter

A wood dominated by oak trees epitomises the traditional idea of an English woodland. This association is no accident as the predominance of oak over large areas of lowland Britain can be traced back to the climax forests of approximately 7000 years ago. Although in the intervening period man has radically altered the landscape, the ancestors of these oak woodlands still remain in places and these mighty trees have certainly not lost their ability to capture our imagination. To learn more about these fascinating woods and their associated animals and plants we made a journey to the heart of the Sussex Weald to visit an area of mixed oak woodland. Our guide for the day was David Streeter, Reader in Ecology at Sussex University and a well-known writer and broadcaster on our countryside.

We met next to the roar of August traffic rushing south to the Sussex coast, but before

The leaves and acorns of a Sessile Oak (*Quercus petraea*). **Note,** however, that although the acorns are sessile, the leaves have auricles at the base which is a character of the Pedunculate Oak (*Quercus robur*).

long we were heading off into the pleasant summer shade of the woodland. The urgency of the birdsong earlier in the year had died down and the quiet of the wood was only periodically broken by the high-pitched calls of tits, which were already moving around in small flocks, and by the busy humming of clusters of hoverflies and bees searching for nectar amongst the glades and sun-dappled branches. As we wound our way down into the heart of the wood David told us of the background to the area.

'The wood we are in today is part of the most wooded region in the whole of the British Isles. Sussex, in fact, is the most heavily wooded county in almost the least wooded country in Europe. Something like 15 per cent of the land here is woodland, whereas the national average is about 8 per cent. Therefore from the point of view of woodland conservation, this is a most important area, certainly in England.

'We are in the middle of the natural region known as the Weald, which is generally taken as being the area enclosed within the encircling rim of the chalk of the North and South Downs and the eastern edge of the Hampshire Downs in the west. It is a very ancient wooded area. The term "weald" itself comes from the Old English, "wald", meaning a forest, and in Anglo Saxon times it was known as "Andredes weald" which is a reference to "Anderida", which was the Roman port of Pevensey and one of the most important coastal forts in this part of the country. The Weald is mentioned in the Anglo Saxon Chronicle for AD 893 and is described as an area of about 120 miles long and 30 miles wide from north to south. The Venerable Bede described it as the haunt of large herds of swine and deer. It was clearly largely an impenetrable area, although modern archaeological and place-names research is showing us that certainly by the latter part of the Saxon period considerable areas had been cleared, largely for swine pastures.

'The central Weald is a very complex area geologically but to put it simply, it consists of an alternating series of sandstones and clays. The Ashdown Sand is the oldest and Ashdown Forest itself occupies the central area of the Weald. This is then followed by the Wadhurst Clay and then the Tunbridge Wells Sand, which is what we are on at the moment. The Tunbridge Wells Sand at this point forms a fairly coarse-grained sandstone and also outcrops as sand-rock. If we were to dig down just here we would come to this solid sand-rock which is only about 30 centimetres beneath the surface. At the moment we are at the highest part of the wood, about 170 metres (550 feet) above sea level, and we shall be walking down the valley onto the Wadhurst Clay with its rather heavier loamy soils. So here we are on sandy acid soils.

'The popular conception of the history of woodlands in this part of the world was that at one time it was one vast expanse of oak forest. I think we have to modify that picture today because research has shown that oak was not the dominant tree over all areas of lowland Britain. But certainly, I suspect this particular area is one where it may well have been. The wood is, in fact, a nature reserve of about 45 hectares (110 acres), managed by the Sussex Trust for Nature Conservation and owned by the National Trust. It has not been actively managed as far as we know for forty or fifty years, although there are small areas of coppiced woodland within it. Most of it, however, consists of old oak standards.'

Although still near the top of the ridge, we had by now made our way into an area dominated by mature oaks. David suggested that we should stop and have a closer look at the trees themselves. We gathered a few leaves and sitting by the side of the path we talked about these stately trees.

'Arguably the oak is the most important plant in Britain because it is the dominant plant of the country's natural climax vegetation. This means, not surprisingly, that it has more species of insect associated with it than any other plant in Britain – well over 300 species are dependent directly on the oak. And that figure only includes those that feed on the leaves and takes no account of the wood boring insects and those that feed on decaying wood. Ecologically speaking therefore it is obviously a very important tree.

'The first thing we have to say is that we have two species of native oak in Britain. Unfortunately they can be rather difficult to distinguish apart. In this wood we have both species and I have collected some examples of each and if we look at the leaves and acorns we should be able to tell the difference between the two. The Common or Pedunculate Oak, *Quercus robur*, has acorns with long stalks or peduncles, hence the name. The leaves of the Pendunculate Oak have no stalks or very short ones and the bases of the leaves have two very small

lobes which stand out at the junction of the leaf and the leaf blade. Also if you turn over the leaf you will see that its underside is completely devoid of hairs. The other species of oak, the Sessile or Durmast Oak, *Quercus petraea*, has acorns which have no peduncles, that is to say they are sessile, again hence the name. The leaves, on the other hand do have stalks, which can be up to one centimetre or more in length, and the base of the leaf blade typically tapers into the leaf stalk. Furthermore, if you look at the undersurface of the leaf you will find that the veins are minutely downy or hairy.

'This all sounds very nice and straightforward but the problem is that when you find an oak you often discover that it is very difficult to decide which species you are looking at. Although the books are very clear on the differences it is not the same at all when you come to look at the trees in the field. The reason for this is argued about,

Sessile or Durmast Oak (*Quercus petraea*) **a habit; b leaf; c acorn. Common or Pedunculate Oak** (*Quercus robor*) **d habit; e bark; f leaf; g acorn.**

but I suppose the obvious conclusion that one comes to is that the two species hybridise. Actually it is very difficult to get oaks to hybridise artificially and it is likely that they only hybridise naturally in the field rather infrequently. The other theory is that the two species are taxonomically very closely related and have separated fairly recently in geological times. The concensus view today, however, is that the explanation for this variability lies in the fact that sometime in the past and, perhaps, to some extent continuing today, the oaks have undergone a special type of hybridisation which is known as 'introgression'. This occurs when the individuals hybridise infrequently and the offspring of the hybrids backcross with the parents. So what results are populations of one or other of the species into which have been incorporated characters of the other species. You therefore tend to get populations where individuals show intermediate characters. But having said that, it is still generally true that over north and west Britain the Sessile Oak is the commoner species, whilst over much of lowland Britain, the Pedunculate Oak is the common one.

'An important ecological principle is that normally speaking where you have two species of organisms which are closely related, they should occupy slightly different habitats, or put another way, very closely related species very rarely have identical ecologies. Yet here we have in this wood the two oaks growing side by side apparently contradicting this – one of the important "dogmas" of ecological theory. This either means that the theory is wrong or alternatively that the oaks are separated ecologically in a way that is not immediately obvious. Let us assume for the moment that the theory is right and look for some differences in the natural history of the two oak species. First one has to point out that their geographical distribution is almost identical – the Pedunculate Oak extends marginally further north and south in Europe than the Sessile. For example, the Pedunculate Oak is found in Sardinia whilst the Sessile Oak reaches as far south as Corsica; they are that close. So to all intents and purposes they have identical geographical distributions. But what about their detailed ecology. The one thing that one can say fairly definitely is that the Pedunculate Oak will tolerate heavier clay soils to a much greater extent than the Sessile Oak. So over much of lowland and

midland Britain where you have heavy clay soils the dominant oak is the Pedunculate. Now, on the other hand, where you have well-drained soils on sandstones you can find both species, but the factor which seems to separate them under those conditions is the general level of soil fertility. Where the soil is more fertile it seems that the Pedunculate has the edge over the Sessile Oak. Conversely, the less fertile the soil, the more likely it is that the Sessile will be the commoner of the two. But the pattern is far from clear. The problem becomes more acute where you get the picture complicated by the appearance of the Beech, *Fagus sylvatica*, which is our other major forest tree, certainly in southern Britain. This tree has an ecology that is similar to the Sessile Oak in that it likes a well-drained soil. It is certainly not confined to limestone and chalk, as some of the books suggest; the Beech simply likes a well-drained soil and so you will find it mixed on soils like the one we are now on, with the two oaks. Areas like the New Forest have almost equal proportions of the two oaks and Beech. However, like the Sessile Oak it will not grow on heavy water-logged soils.

'One factor which has complicated our understanding of the ecology of the two oaks is that they have been of prime importance to man for timber and so he has artificially changed their apparent ecology by hundreds of years of planting and felling. So it may no longer be possible wholly to interpret their ecologies properly, simply because we are looking at an artificial distribution.

'As far as the uses of oak are concerned, the Pedunculate Oak has always been the most favoured for timber. Paradoxically, one reason for this is that it has the most crooked branches and thus the most crooked timber of the two! One of the prime uses in the past for oak timber has been in the building both of houses and ships, and one of the things that the medieval builders needed were those lovely right-angled bends for supplying the "knees" and "crutches" for supporting roof timbers and so on. If you look at this oak in front of us you can see that the branches are full of these right-angled bends, whereas the typical branches of the Sessile Oak tend to be straighter.

'As far as planting is concerned, from a pure husbandry point of view the Pedunculate Oak is again preferred as its acorns store better. The trees that you often see growing by themselves in the open are usually

Pedunculate Oaks. Incidentally, as they are not hemmed in by other trees, the crowns of these hedgerow or parkland trees tend to be more open. Indeed, one thing you can do when you go into a woodland, which you think might be ancient woodland or one that has been there a long time, is to look at the crowns of the trees, if they are narrow then you can be fairly sure that they have grown up in competition with other individuals.

'If you want to see the finest oak woods in Europe then unfortunately you have to look outside Britain as we do not have any wholly untouched oak woods. The best woodlands of Pedunculate Oak are probably in some of the river valleys of Yugoslavia, while the best Sessile Oak woods are probably in parts of eastern France.

'We are here in late August and if you look at the oak at this time of year the one thing that strikes you more than anything else is that a lot of the leaves have virtually nothing left of them. It so happens that this year it looks as if between 10 and 15 per cent of the leaves have been eaten – some years you can get a devastating defoliation. This is simply a feature of the fact that the oak is palatable to an enormous array of herbivorous insects, particularly their larvae. By this time of the year most of these insects have matured and the predation pressure is off. Therefore what we can see is probably the maximum amount of defoliation for this year. Interestingly, if you look carefully at the oaks you will find that there are some leaves which have been hardly eaten at all. This is because in July many of the oaks produce a second crop of leaves on non-woody shoots. This is called lammas-growth, after Lammastide, one of the old country festivals, which occurs on the 1st of August. The distinction between the first spring leaves and this lammas-growth can be very dramatic; it is best seen in July. This means that even if the oak tree was severely defoliated in the spring, if it produced this second crop of leaves, it would not wholly lose its year's production. However, it would actually be wrong to argue that the oak, and, indeed, other trees that produce this growth, actually evolved this as a mechanism to overcome the effects of heavy predation loss early in the year. However, there is little doubt that the effect is to provide the tree with a "second string" to its annual "photosynthesis" bow!

'Whilst we are looking at the leaves there are two other features which can be very noticeable at this time of the year. One of them is the large number of different galls that you find. Perhaps the commonest gall on mature oaks is the spangle gall which you find on the undersurface of the leaf. These are little circular pustules which vary in diameter from two millimetres up to about five millimetres. Like a lot of galls on the oak, they are caused by a gall wasp belonging to the family Cynipidae. There are more species of gall wasp on oak than I know of on any other plant in Britain – around thirty species. Galls are not animal tissue but are the result of the plant's response to the invasion of gall-causing organisms, in this case, a wasp. They are a form of controlled cancer, if you like. An abnormal growth within which the larva of the gall wasp develops. This particular one that we can see here – the spangle gall – is the result of eggs that would have been laid by the female wasp in July and there is one caterpillar per spangle. These will continue to grow throughout the late summer, until the autumn when they will fall off – they usually fall off before the leaf itself – and the larva continues its life cycle still within the protection of the spangle but now within the added safety of the leaf litter. Over winter it pupates, hatching out in the spring as an adult, but all those emerging then will be female wasps. These female wasps will then fly up to the young flower buds of the oak and lay their eggs. These produce little round galls in the male catkins that look like currants. So next April you should have a look at the male catkins and you might find these reddish-yellow currant-sized galls. The larvae pupate inside the galls and eventually hatch out in early summer producing both males and females. The females, after they have been fertilized, will lay their eggs on the undersurface of the leaf, producing these spangle galls. Therefore you have two alternating generations – one that produces males and females in mid-summer and another in early spring that produces females only that lay eggs without fertilization.

'There are several species of these spangle gall wasp, three of which are quite common. This one is caused by a little beast called *Neuroterus quercusbaccarum*, which nicely obeys the rule that the smaller the animal, the longer the name! We were talking about the ecological theory that says that closely related species do not compete with each

other and here we have the possibility of three species of *Neuroterus* making spangles on the same oak! However, if you study them carefully you find that one species is commoner at the top of the crown, another around the edge and the third in the middle. Occasionally you will even find more than one species on the same leaf, in which case the different species partition up the leaf between them so that one species is commoner up the middle of the leaf, another produces spangles round the edge and a third, perhaps, at the tip.

'Other familiar galls that you can find are the oak apple gall, which does look, in fact, like an apple, and the "hop" or "artichoke" gall.

'Another feature which may be noticeable at this time of year is mildew on the leaves. This is a fungus disease (*Microsphaera alphitoides*) which is often common on the lammas growth and on oak coppice. Some years are worse than others and this year happens to be fairly bad.

'Let us follow the food chain through for a little while. What exactly is it that defoliates the trees so heavily? Well, I have already said that it was estimated some years ago, that well over 300 species of insect feed on oaks but again, it is an important ecological principle that you only normally have a small number of common species and a very large number of rarer species. A good example of that are the oak tree herbivores, as 90 per cent of damage that we can see here has been caused by only two species of moth. Therefore out of this great array of 300 or so species of beetles, bugs and moths, nearly all the defoliation has been caused by two species: the Winter Moth, *Operophtera brummata*, which will feed on a whole range of trees including fruit trees where it can be a pest; and the Green Oak Moth, *Tortrix viridana*, which only feeds on the oak. The Winter Moth has a very interesting life history – it seems to have the rather unintelligent habit of emerging in the middle of November. The females are wingless, just to make the whole thing more bizarre, but the males are winged. The females emerge from their pupae in the ground during the winter and then climb the trunk of the tree where they mate with the males at night. They then climb further up, laying their eggs towards the tips of the branches or in crevices in the bark. The caterpillars emerge in the spring just as the leaves are breaking.

'The Green Oak Moth, on the other hand,

Above **Beech** (*Fagus sylvatica*) **a habit; b bark; c spring shoot with flowers; d mature leaf; e nuts.**

Below **Ash** (*Fraxinus excelsior*) **a habit; b bark; c flowering twig; d male flower; e leaf; f fruits.**

Opposite top **Leaves of Pedunculate Oak after a season's predation. Over 300 species of insect are dependent directly on oaks, but most of the defoliation is carried out by the larvae of just two species: the Green Oak Moth and the Winter Moth.**

Opposite bottom **Spangle galls on the underside of an oak leaf. These are caused by a minute gall wasp,** *Neuroterus.*

95

has a more conventional life history. The caterpillars hatch just as the leaves unfold in early spring after overwintering as eggs. The adult moths appear in July and are quite small but do have forewings that are a most glorious emerald green colour.

'By May there is this enormous population of caterpillars feeding in the canopy. I can remember walking in the wood earlier in the year and it sounded as though it was raining. In fact, what I could hear was the caterpillar "frass" falling out of the trees and beating the vegetation beneath. When I looked at some of the leaves close to the ground, they were absolutely black with these caterpillar droppings. Following the food-chain through, this huge population is itself food for the woodland insect-eating birds particularly the tits and warblers. Interestingly, it is possible to estimate the size of this vast population of caterpillars.

'First, you have to calculate how much a single caterpillar eats. This you can do by taking some home and keeping them in tubes and measuring the amount of "frass" produced by each caterpillar in a 24 hour period. You then go back to the wood and lay a sheet beneath a tree and 24 hours later return and sweep up all the frass. This heap of caterpillar droppings is then weighed and if this is divided by the weight produced by one caterpillar, you have an estimate of the number of caterpillars in the tree above the sheet. People who spend their lives carrying out this kind of research are called "production ecologists".

'There is a link here with one of the major problems of oakwood ecology – the apparent lack of young trees. All the trees around here are roughly between 100 and 200 years old and there is very little apparent regeneration. This is something which worries foresters enormously and it is worth examining the possible reasons for this.

'All sorts of suggestions to explain this lack of regeneration have been put forward by ecologists but it is now generally agreed that the main cause is one which intriguingly links up the history of the management of these oak woods with their own internal natural history. One of the things you come across is that oak seedlings appear to occur virtually anywhere except an oak wood – you find them in your garden, on heathland, by roadsides and so on. It is much less frequent to find them under a dense woodland canopy. The reason for this is partly to do with the caterpillar story, as any seedling that comes

up and produces half a dozen luscious young leaves is going to be literally fallen upon in May by the hoard of caterpillars that have come adrift from the canopy above. So there is a reason why we cannot see many seedlings under an oak tree – they simply would not survive the predation. The question that then follows quite naturally is, has not that always been the case, so what circumstances make it so critical now? Well, under natural forest conditions you would have a completely mixed age-distribution of trees giving everything from saplings and young trees to mature trees and great gaps in the canopy caused by fallen trees. Where there are these natural gaps and clearings regeneration is able to take place. Now, an oak tree will live up to 350 years under normal conditions, and you would not expect natural gaps in the canopy to appear until the trees were at least that age. Now, most of our woods have been cut in the past and have generally regenerated from some fixed date in the past. This wood, for instance, we have looked at carefully and know that most of the trees are between 50 and 170 years old, making them middle-aged from the point of view of an oak tree. But more importantly, because they are all broadly the same age you do not have any natural gaps in the canopy and therefore there is little regeneration.

'It has been argued that a contributing factor is that the acorn crop is failing. However, if that is so, it must be largely for climatic reasons. Therefore, one is saying that the dominant plant of Britain's climatic climax is failing to regenerate itself because the climate is wrong. This is obviously not a tenable argument and although the crop does vary from year to year it is perfectly adequate.

'Another factor which affects the success of the acorn crop is that they are fed on by birds and mammals. One bird in particular does have an influence on the acorn crop and that is the Woodpigeon. This bird is primarily a forest species and unlike a lot of our native birds it is a true herbivore and has a crop like a pheasant or a partridge. It is therefore a grazing animal and under natural forest conditions it feeds on the ground in woodland clearings, and come the autumn it has a craving for a feast of acorns to liven its diet. But, of course, you again will ask if it has always done this in the past, why should it have such an effect now? Well, if one wanted to encapsulate in one sentence what man has done to the English landscape one could say that he has turned it from a forest with small areas of woodland clearing into a vast great woodland clearing with small areas of forest! Therefore any animal which is able to take advantage of these clearings has been enormously favoured by this change, and the Woodpigeon is a good example. What is more, man has improved the quality of the food grown in this big "woodland clearing" and pigeons take full advantage of this, as anyone with a cabbage patch will know to their cost. The Woodpigeon, then has increased its population dramatically as a result of man's activities and now, a far bigger population than the forest would naturally have been able to support still comes swooping in during the autumn for its annual feast of acorns. So here is a subtle and indirect way in which man has, perhaps, influenced the regeneration of the oak woods.

'Another feature which has changed over the years is the influence of large mammals on the forest. Most of our woods no longer have the great populations of Red Deer described by Bede. Nor do we have any Wild Boar left and they would have had an influence on the germination of the acorns. For, as well as eating them, they also churned up the forest floor while they rooted around, providing ideal conditions for germination. Many woods of the high Weald were used as swine pastures by the coastal manors and we know, for example, from studying Saxon documents and other evidence, that they were used primarily as pasture up until the Seventh Century.

'I suppose the pay off to all this is that in order to perpetuate the forest all that needs to be ensured is that each oak produces one offspring that will survive to maturity during its life. Try and imagine the number of acorns that one mature tree produces throughout its life – it is absolutely vast. It has been calculated that for each tree to produce one acorn to maturity the probability of acorn survival need be only something of the order of 1 in 18 million. So perhaps, if you don't see too many seedlings developing it is not quite as much a problem as some of the foresters believe. Also it is important to consider that naturally an oak takes 350 years to mature rather than 100–150 years, which is when the forester would regard a tree to be old.

The ground vegetation of the wood on sandy soils is dominated by Bracken in mid-summer. This fern, unlike many others, can colonise the drier areas as it is able to spread vegetatively by means of its underground rhizomes.

Silver Birch (*Betula pendula*) **a habit; b bark; c leaf; d flowering twig with male and female catkins; e scale; f nutlet. Downy Birch** (*Betula pubescens*) **g habit; h bark; i leafy twig with fruiting catkins; j scale; k nutlet.**

trees around here you can see that they have many dead branches on them, which would be anathema to a forester. But they are important to a large number of our rarest invertebrates, particularly beetles, some of which are specific to this habitat of dead wood on standing trees. So ironically, it is best to act in a positively negative way if you want to achieve this type of mature woodland.'

Having had a good look at the trees we then moved off further into the wood and as we walked down David told us about the ground flora.

'One feature about woodlands that can tell us a great deal about the soil on which they are growing as well as the ecology generally, is the ground vegetation. And in these sandstone woods of the central Weald there are four plants which dominate the ground flora. Unfortunately, at this time of year, all we can see is the one, as we are surrounded by shoulder high Bracken. But if you were to come earlier in the year you would see three other species as well – Bluebells, Bramble and surprisingly enough, Honeysuckle. Four species which are all common British woodland plants. Totally unremarkable one might think, but if you told, say, a Japanese ecologist, that you had just come from an area with these four species he would say that you must have been in an oak woodland somewhere in Europe west of the Black Forest, south of Denmark and north of Spain. What's more he would have told you what type of soil you had been on. The reason that he could be so precise is the presence of the Bluebell, which although common here is globally an extremely restricted species. You do not find it outside the broad boundaries I have just mentioned and in Britain we are at the heart of its distribution range. The Honeysuckle is almost as restricted, but it goes a little further east and south. The Bracken, on the other hand, is one of the most widespread plants in the world but it is a useful indicator of acid, well-drained soils. It can be a very dominant plant, as it is here. It was probably originally a woodland glade species but as the woods became opened out it has been able to become even more dominant. It does not rely on sexual reproduction like most of the other ferns, but almost always spreads by underground rhizomes.

'The other interesting fact about Bracken is that, unlike the leaves of oak, it looks as if nothing eats it at all. It is said that it is a very

If you are managing an area of woodland as natural high forest the management prescription, interestingly, is to do nothing – one of the few occasions where this is true. This is to enable the older trees to fully mature and eventually die, opening out the canopy and providing dead and decaying wood. The importance of this dead wood in natural history terms is enormous. I believe it has been estimated that as much as 25 per cent of the British fauna, which it must be remembered is primarily forest dwelling, is in some way dependent on this dead or decaying wood. If you look at some of the dull plant from an entomologist's point of view, but this is only partly true. You don't have many insects feeding on it early in the year because the Bracken contains a lot of poisonous substances, including cyanides. But the cyanide content of the leaves declines as the season progresses so more animals feed on the Bracken later in the year, which is the opposite of the oak. The poisonous tannins in the oak build up as the season progresses so most of its predation occurs at the beginning of the season. If you look carefully at the Bracken fronds you will find that there are quite a few caterpillars feeding on them. These are mostly the larvae of sawflies, the preponderance of which is a peculiar feature of Bracken. Also at this time of the year you can find the tips

The stream at the bottom of the wood cuts its way through the porous sandstone under a dense wood-land canopy which has enabled this humid micro-habitat to retain its links with a climatic period that was prevalent over much of Britain 5000 years ago.

Typical view of the wood with the lichen encrusted oaks presiding over a dense ground cover.

of the fronds curled up in a ball. This is a gall caused by a fly related to the house fly called *Chirosia parvicornis*. The other thing to look out for in late summer are little black cigar-shaped galls which can be found on the undersurface at the tips. This is another gall caused by a gall midge which is more or less specific to Bracken, called *Dasyneura filicina*.

'Here we are in a more open part of the wood and one of the things that you would expect to see in the clearings, is tree regeneration. In normal forest conditions you will find a sequence of tree species coming into the gap in the canopy leading up to the final re-establishment of oak or Beech, or whatever the dominant tree happens to be. The tree on this soil which functions as a "nurse crop" for the oak is the birch. Birches grow well on these infertile, rather well-drained soils. If this were a more fertile loamy soil the Ash would have been the first to colonise the clearing. Now, one of the things about the birch, which in a way is similar to the oak, is that we have two rather similar species – the Silver Birch, *Betula pendula*, and the Downy Birch, *Betula pubescens*. Here I have a shoot of each and if we look at the

young twigs, those of the Downy Birch, as the name suggests, are dull in colour because they are covered with a soft down. The twigs of the Silver Birch, on the other hand are a dark brown polished colour and are covered with little warts. Also, the shapes of the leaves are quite distinct, as the leaf tips of the Silver Birch are far more attenuated than those of the Downy Birch. Also the toothing on the margin of the Silver Birch leaf is much coarser and more irregular than that of the Downy Birch.

'Unfortunately, again like the oaks, you do find intermediates between the two. However, the reason for this is a little more clear than in the oaks. It seems that the Downy Birch arose as a result of a cross between the Silver Birch and an east European species, which is not found in Britain called *Betula humilis*. Now most hybrids are infertile but they can produce a fertile offspring if they undergo a doubling in the chromosome number. This is probably what happened and in effect a new species was formed – the Downy Birch. It is what the geneticists would call an allotetraploid and being a tetraploid species with a larger chromosome number they tend to be more variable than the "parent" diploid species. So the trick is – if in doubt, call it a Downy Birch. One word of caution, however, although the Silver Birch is generally a larger tree and is usually the one with pendulous branches, both the Silver and the Downy Birch can have the beautiful silver bark. The Silver Birch has a more continental distribution than the Downy and in this country you find that the Downy is quite often the commoner one on wet organic soils of the north and west. Where you have birch growing on chalk it will almost always be the Silver Birch.

'Both birches produce an enormous number of seeds each year and these germinate very readily, so it is quick to take advantage of any clearings. It does not form a very dense canopy and lets in enough light to allow young oak or Beech seedlings to develop yet, on the other hand, it makes enough shade to keep the ground flora from swamping the young seedlings.

'Birches have a large number of insects associated with them but not as many as the oaks. Generally speaking, the more common the tree and the longer its ecological history in an area, the larger will be the number of species that feed on it. There are two families of trees which are an exception to this and which have a larger number of insect species than you would expect, and those are the Rosaceae, which includes hawthorns, crab apples, Sloe and so on, and the other is the willow family – Salicaceae, which includes the willows, poplars and sallows. The converse to the general hypothesis is certainly true – that trees which have only recently been introduced have very few, if any, insects associated with them. Examples of this are the Sycamore and the Sweet Chestnut. A lot of evergreens also have few insects, for example, the Holly and the Yew. But this is not always the case as Scots Pine has a very large number of insects dependent on it.

'I should say at this point that relatively few insect groups have actually evolved the ability to eat leaves. We tend to think of one or two garden pests and imagine the world to be populated by a vast variety of insects feeding on leaves but if you look at all the thirty or so orders of insects, very few have evolved efficient means of feeding on leaves. The caterpillars of butterflies and moths, the larvae and adults of some beetles, gall wasps and sawflies and the bugs, have all exploited this food source. But that is only four orders. If you think about it, it is a very

hazardous existence as you have to be able to hang on to a pretty precarious perch in all kinds of adverse conditions. Not only that but you have to be able to eat through a leaf that is covered with a waxy waterproof layer which can be pretty tough. Add to all this the fact that the plants themselves have developed all sorts of mechanisms to combat insect predation, such as poisons, thick cuticles and all manner of thorns, spines and prickles, and you can see why so few insects have evolved to exploit them.'

We were now down at the bottom of the slope and were in a very different landscape. The old track way we had followed was now no longer open but surrounded by steep sided banks. The air had become more humid and noticeably cooler but the exciting thing was that the ground vegetation had gradually been changing and the dominance of the Bracken in the higher reaches had been slowly replaced by an increasing variety of different ferns. A stream was winding its way along the valley bottom and we sat beside this while David told us something of the history of this landscape.

'We have come down to the bottom of the valley and are now beside a stream which is running between great outcrops of the sandstone, which is producing some very steep sides, and the stream itself is full of sandstone boulders. The one thing that strikes you is that the whole atmosphere has changed, it feels cooler and damper. In other words it feels a bit like the climate you might find in a Welsh oak wood rather than one in Sussex. This is because of a special feature of these central Weald woodlands which sets them apart from most other woods in lowland Britain. The extraordinary thing is that there are a large number of plants and animals here which occur normally only in the extreme west of the British Isles. All this obviously requires some sort of explanation.

'The story seems to be that at one time somewhere between 5 000 BC and 3 000 BC, the whole of Britain and western Europe experienced a climate that was a great deal wetter than at present. This is called the Atlantic Period. In other words, the whole of western Europe was experiencing a climate similar to that which Ireland experiences today. Not only was it wetter but it was also warmer. At that time, then, species that are now restricted to the extreme western seaboard had a much wider distribution. Since then the climate has become less oceanic and many species have become more restricted in their distribution but here in this one part of lowland Britain some of the species have persisted. Why is this? The answer seems to be in the very peculiar topography that we see here. These very steep narrow stream ravines faced with this very porous sandstone rock, which functions like a sponge, means that it is permanently wet and the atmosphere is constantly humid. Not only that, but this area has a rather peculiar ecological history in that until relatively recently this was still predominantly forest. Large areas were cleared probably around the Fourteenth Century, much later than the rest of lowland Britain, and even then it still remained one of the most heavily wooded parts of Britain. So these deep ravines have been permanently covered over in summer with a dense woodland canopy resulting in a micro-climate similar to that of western Britain.

'On this bank here we have the best example amongst the plants, of this particular phenomenon – the Hay-scented

Hay-scented Fern (*Dryopteris aemula*); a classic example of a plant with a disjunct 'oceanic' distribution, surviving as a relict in the Wealden oak woods.

Fern, *Dryopteris aemula*. It has lovely crisp fronds that look like big parsley-shaped leaves. It is one of Europe's rarest ferns and has a very "oceanic" distribution, being found in south-west Ireland, south-west England, the western edge of Scotland, western Spain, the mountains of the Azores and Madeira and here, in the Weald. It has this extraordinary "disjunct" distribution. It is doing very well this year but interestingly it is only growing on the north-facing side of the valley, so it is very selective even in this, its chosen niche. The humid atmosphere is supporting a superb variety of ferns. Below us are Hard Ferns and some Polypody. The Polypody is interesting because it is almost the only British plant, other than some mosses, which is habitually epiphytic. There are Male Ferns and Broad and Narrow Buckler Ferns as well as Borrer's Male Ferns and the delicate Lady Fern. We have even some Mountain Fern which is more characteristic of the fern meadows of the western Highlands!'

'So here we have a combination of ecology, archaeology, historical geography,

Hard Fern (*Blechnum spicant*); **a woodland fern of sandy soils. In the centre of the rosette of sterile fronds is an erect fertile frond.**

and pollen analysis all contributing information to explain this fascinating story. People keep turning up new things to strengthen the picture – a water beetle was found not far from here, about ten years ago, which was only previously known from Scotland and Scandinavia. It is flightless so it is unlikely to have arrived recently and is probably another example of a relict species.'

I must admit that I was rather amazed at the variety that was all around us but the dank atmosphere was beginning to creep through to our bones so we headed for a more open area nearby which, although it was wooded, was very different from the oak woods further up the slope. David explained.

'There are just one or two small areas of coppice in this wood and, here in the Weald, the most valuable and characteristic is Sweet Chestnut coppice. These are very different from the old primary woodland coppices of East Anglia where you have a mix of species. The ones here have been deliberately planted as a coppice crop. Sweet Chestnut is not a native to Britain as it was brought here by the Romans. I would suspect that they imported it not for its wood, but for the nuts, as in those days nuts were an important part of everyone's diet. However, since about the Seventeenth Century it has been extensively planted as a coppice species. Being southern European in origin it will only grow well in southern Britain and it also likes a well-drained soil. It is slower growing than Hazel and is cut on a 13–15 year rotation, forming beautiful long coppice poles. Today, it is the only hardwood coppice that is still really an economic proposition. It is used primarily for fencing and in this part of the country was also important in providing poles for that most important of British crops – hops!

'There is another type of coppice in the wood and if we walk back up to the ridge we will have a look at that.'

We made our way back through the wood past the ferns and the towering oaks until we came to an area where the trees looked rather small and stunted. It was obviously a different type of coppice to the vigorous Sweet Chestnuts in the valley bottom.

'This is an interesting feature. It is oak coppice which, in fact, is more characteristic of western Britain. One of the reasons that we have it here, is that we are now right on top of the ridge again and the sandstone is very close to the surface which limits the quality of the oak, which prefers a reasonable depth of soil. Oak is very deep rooting which is one of the reasons it does not do well on chalk which typically forms shallow soils. When the management of the wood was deter-

The bank by this old woodland path is covered in mosses which have taken advantage of the fact that it is too steep to be covered in leaf litter, thus enabling them access to the filtered sunlight.

mined, it was obviously decided that because of this shallow soil, standard trees would not do well and so the oak was coppiced. If you look carefully you can see that the branches are coming up from old stools. It has not been coppiced now for some time and it is looking rather overgrown.

'What was it coppiced for? Well, the wood would have been used for all kinds of purposes but particularly it was used for charcoal. One of the things we must remember is that we are slap in the middle of what was the Wealden iron industry region. It is difficult to believe that 300 years ago this was the industrial heart of Britain, together with the Forest of Dean and the Lake District. The iron industry used an enormous amount of charcoal and to be of any use the oak had to be coppiced. It would have been cut on a twenty or thirty year rotation as it is slow growing.

'Another thing that it was grown for is its bark. Right up until the late Eighteenth Century leather was, after textiles, Britain's most important product in terms of value, and 90 per cent of the hides were tanned with oak bark. The amount that was used was phenomenal: for the period 1810 to 1815, England alone produced 90 000 tons of oak bark for tanning. The tannin content of the bark declines with age so they did not want anything too old and would therefore coppice the oak and strip the bark after, say, twenty years. This process of stripping the stems was called "flawing" and they used a special "flawing knife" for this. The bulk of the industry ceased in the 1830s when bark began to be imported from abroad, particularly from France after the Napoleonic wars. I can remember talking to the present Lord of the Manor's Reeve on Ashdown Forest about twenty years ago and he said he could remember his father, when he was a lad, talking about men going to the forest and flawing the oaks.'

Today the bark of the coppiced branches are covered with dense clusters of lichens and would now certainly be spared the flawing knife. We returned to the main path which had been worn down over the centuries by the comings and goings of countless generations of foresters and travellers. We had been the only people in the wood all afternoon, the birds were still foraging in the tree tops and as we approached the road the silence was quickly swamped by the familiar rush of cars. It had certainly been a fascinating walk, as David Streeter had clearly shown us that there was so much more to do than simply ambling along occasionally naming a plant or an animal here and there.

The bark of this low coppiced oak is covered in a rich layer of lichens which testify to the humid atmosphere and the relatively unpolluted air.

A Woodland Walk in Autumn

Step on the underground at Oxford Circus, take the Central Line and a mere eighteen stops later you can start to explore Epping Forest, which is as important a part of London's history as the Tower itself. I did exactly that when I went on my first 'fungus foray' with the London Natural History Society. Autumn is without doubt one of the best times of year to visit any woodland. The mass of the trees shuts out the chill wind and the sun shafting down through the golden leaves gives a warm feeling, even if there is frost in the air. Then there are the fungi, or at least their fruiting bodies, for the main butt of their feeding hyphae are hidden deep down in the litter and the rotting wood. Paul Moxey is the Warden of the Epping Forest Conservation Centre. In this chapter he shows us some of the history of this former Royal Forest as well as some of its present wildlife.

Epping Forest in the autumn – a rich mixture of wildlife and colour.

Information

In a deciduous wood one of the major transformations that occurs in the autumn is the shedding of leaves by the trees. When this happens in your garden probably your first thought is to sweep the leaves up and burn them as they are doing nobody any good, least of all the trees. But this is far from the truth. Even in the dense toxic leaf-litter of a Beech wood careful examination will show that the leaves are being broken down by thousands of small animals and plants. These decomposers are extremely important in the survival of the woodland as they enable the nutrients stored in the leaf-litter or decaying wood to be recycled through the soil thus enabling the trees as well as animals to continue to thrive. This league of tiny organisms includes a wide range of types from woodlice and slugs to millipedes and spiders as well as microscopic bacteria, but one of the most important members of this group is the fungi.

Fungi

Fungi are a large and important class of organisms with a wide range of forms. They are peculiar in having a mode of nutrition similar to that of animals, whilst their structure is more akin to that of plants. Thus, they are dependent for their sustenance, and so for their source of energy for growth, on complex carbon compounds manufactured by other organisms. These they obtain by growing on the living or dead bodies of these organisms. In contrast, the great majority of plants absorb energy from the sun's radiation and employ this to build up complex carbon compounds from carbon dioxide in the air, water and minerals. Fungi consist in the main of thin, usually branching filaments, called hyphae, made up of tubular cells placed end to end. These hyphae grow through the material from which nutrients are being obtained, such as soil, wood or other plant material or, occasionally, living or dead animals. They form a very fine, tenuous, loose and cobweb-like weft called the mycelium, which is normally barely visible to the naked eye except when grouped into cords. The mycelium is the body of the fungus and is roughly equivalent to the roots, stem and leaves of a flowering plant, but is ordinarily hidden from view in the soil or other medium in which the fungus is growing.

What are commonly referred to as mushrooms or toadstools are, in fact, the reproductive bodies, and are the only parts that can normally be seen. They are equivalent to the flowers and fruit of a flowering plant and they produce the spores by which the fungus is disseminated. The spores may be likened to seeds but do not contain an embryonic plant and, usually consist instead, of a single cell. They are also much smaller, being invisible to the naked eye since they range in size, according to species, from 0·001 to 0·025 millimetres (1 to 25 microns) long. These spores are often produced in very large numbers, a single fruit-body of the Common Mushroom producing 16000 million, and are usually liberated into the air to be carried away by air currents. On landing on a suitable spot, the spore

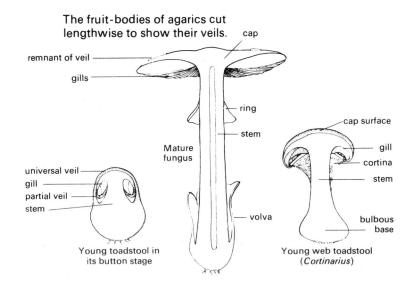

The fruit-bodies of agarics cut lengthwise to show their veils.

cap

remnant of veil

gills

ring

stem

Mature fungus

volva

cap surface

gill

cortina

stem

bulbous base

universal veil

gill

partial veil

stem

Young toadstool in its button stage

Young web toadstool (*Cortinarius*)

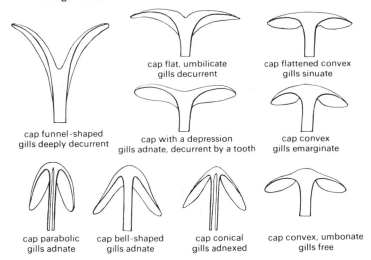

Longitudinal sections of caps to show terms used for their shape and gill attachment.

cap flat, umbilicate
gills decurrent

cap flattened convex
gills sinuate

cap funnel-shaped
gills deeply decurrent

cap with a depression
gills adnate, decurrent by a tooth

cap convex
gills emarginate

cap parabolic
gills adnate

cap bell-shaped
gills adnate

cap conical
gills adnexed

cap convex, umbonate
gills free

germinates and a hypha grows out and branches to form a mass of mycelium.

Many fungi have fruit-bodies that are minute and their structure can only be made out by using a lens or a microscope. They are often referred to as microfungi and they include the yeasts, moulds, mildews, rusts, smuts, and so on. The larger or macrofungi are those whose fruit-bodies can easily be seen by the naked eye and it is these that are called the toadstools and mushrooms.

(Extract from *Hamlyn Nature Guides : Mushrooms and Toadstools* by Ronald Rayner)

Mycorrhizas

When walking in woodland particularly during the autumn you may notice that some fungi keep cropping up under the same species of tree. For example, Orange Birch-boletus, *Leccinum versipelle*, is found almost solely under birches, as is the familiar *Amanita muscaria*. Whilst some species of *Russula* seem to be found most frequently under oak or Beech trees. This association between some types of fungi and trees is called mycorrhizal. Each involves a definite relationship between the fungus and the tree, since the fungal mycelium, as it grows, actually infects the smaller tree roots. These soon become distorted, with a characteristic swollen and much branched appearance. Such fungus-root structures are termed mycorrhizas. Each is enclosed in a dense sheath of hyphae, some of which penetrate between the outer cells of the root. It is assumed by most mycologists that the association is a symbiotic one, in other words, of mutual benefit to both organisms concerned. The tree stores manufactured starch and sugars in the roots and these can be absorbed by the fungus. This in turn is particularly efficient at absorbing mineral salts from the soil and presumably the fungal component passes the salts on to the cells of the tree roots. Since there may be a shortage of these salts in forest soils, especially nitrates, such transfer is extremely valuable to trees. Over fifty years ago it was shown that seedlings of pine and spruce would grow normally in poor soils only when they had developed mycorrhizas, and uninfected seedlings died. It has actually proved possible to induce mycorrhizal roots in pine seedlings by adding mycelium from species of *Boletus, Amanita* and other fungi.

Autumn 'fungus forays' are now a common part in the yearly calendar of meetings of most local Naturalists' Trusts and can prove an enjoyable way of discovering these unusual plants. If you are intending to pick any for consumption it is extremely advisable that you go along with an expert as there are some common species that are very poisonous. Most woods have a selection of recognisable mushrooms and toadstools growing in them, but generally it is the ancient woods that have the best variety, particularly if they contain dead and rotting wood. Some notable examples are Savernake Forest in Wiltshire; the oakwoods of the Weald; Burnham Beeches, Buckinghamshire and Windsor Forest, Berkshire, as well as Epping Forest.

A Woodland Walk in Autumn
with
Paul Moxey

To appreciate the natural history of any habitat it should be visited throughout the year. Woodlands, in particular, lend themselves to this as the seasons are starkly contrasted. What could be more different than a spring wood carpeted in a wash of Bluebells and the deep russet and gold tones of an autumn Beech wood with the dry leaf litter crackling under foot? Yet these aspects are part of the same yearly cycle of regeneration and decomposition.

This walk takes us out into the autumn air through one of Britain's most popular woodland areas – Epping Forest. Here we found not only the colourful fungi that characterise our woods at this time of year but also the very real fact that our present woods are shaped by a much larger continuing cycle of change influenced by long-term variations in climate and the changing ways of man. Our guide for the day was Paul Moxey, Warden of the Epping Forest Conservation Centre at High Beach. We started our walk in front of the centre on an area of open grassland bordered by car parks and Beech wood. Paul described the scene.

'We have started our walk at one of the more popular regions of Epping Forest. It is really a "honeypot" area with good access by road and many public amenities including car parks and pubs. It is interesting that we are standing on open grassland as, although this is popularly thought of as essentially woodland, there are quite large open areas within the forest. Epping Forest is the largest remaining tract of the Royal Forest of Essex and covers 6000 acres but only about 4000 acres are woodland, the rest is this open grassland or heath and has been for centuries.

'If we have a close look at the plant composition of this patch we will be able to see two important things about it. The plant here, amongst the grasses, is Heath Bedstraw which is a common constituent of acid grasslands and heathy areas. It has tiny white flowers, which can be seen in midsummer. So we can say that here the soils are reasonably acidic; geologists have established that the forest sits on a ridge that is capped with sands and gravels overlying clay, which flanks the valleys. Over there is another indicator of acid soils – Wood Sage. That is interesting as it ties in with the other feature that I was going to show you. If you look along the edges of this open area you can see oak seedlings growing up. Now,

this is a reflection of the current lack of grazing pressure on these open areas and they are now being invaded by scrub such as this and also birches and Hawthorn. Grazing is an important element in the history of these woods as, in addition to using the wood for firewood, it was a hunting forest and large herds of deer would have roamed this area. Today very few deer survive having been driven away by disturbance from the public. Also, it has always been common land and local people have the right to graze their cattle on it. This right still exists but the practice has declined considerably recently. The effect of fewer deer and cattle has been compounded since the 1950s with the decimation of the Rabbit population as a result of myxomatosis.

'It is very difficult to overcome this invasion of scrub as the physical removal of the scrub is, by itself, not sufficient to retain the character of the original grassland. The actual species composition changes as the coarser grasses move in and the former diversity of plant species is lost. It is possible to partially overcome this by cutting the grass mechanically but then, of course, you have to take away the cut grass as it will build up the nutrients in the soil. In some areas it is still possible to come across stands of Heather, which is another plant of acid soils and used to be far commoner here when greater grazing pressure kept the scrub back.'

As we walked across to the edge of some woodland, Paul recounted something of the history of the forest.

'We know from pollen records taken from valley bogs in the Forest that there has been continuous woodland on this ridge since at least Neolithic times and this suggests that there has been wood here since the last Ice Age. However, the original forest cover was not what it is today, but was a mixture of Pedunculate Oak and Small-leaved Lime. It probably stayed as that right through to the Ninth Century A.D. when these two dominant species suddenly declined. There was then an upsurge in birch and later in Hornbeam and Beech. This suggests that there was a clearance of the original forest and an invasion of the clearings by birches. This approximate date coincides with the Anglo-Saxon settlement in the area. It looks very much as though they came up the Thames, up the Lea and Roding Rivers on either side of the forest ridge and settled along the river banks. Many of the place-names of East London

The woodland floor in autumn covered in a russet-coloured carpet of Beech leaves. This is not the end of the yearly cycle as these fallen leaves will be broken down by an army of decomposers and will eventually help to provide a rich mulch for next year's growth.

One of Epping's pollarded Beeches. The branches would have traditionally been cut every fifteen years but the trees now have to contend with at least a hundred years' growth. Some are now collapsing under the strain, as you can see on the opposite page.

canopy allowing light to get to the forest floor and encouraging growth under the trees. It also allowed more rain to reach the forest floor – as much as 40 per cent of the rain is intercepted normally by the leaf canopy – which meant increased leaching of the soil and eventually the formation of a podsol in areas. Beech appears to have moved in on these light soils with the birch providing a 'nurse' crop. So we can see that indirectly man has affected the tree composition of the forest and his influence is still considerable as we shall see.

'The pollarding continued right through until 1878, except for various sections, as, for example, around Waltham Abbey where pollarding ceased in the Seventeenth Century. In 1871 there was a court case between the local commoners and the Lord of the Manor, the outcome of which was that he was prosecuted for illegally fencing off the forest and preventing the commoners from cutting wood. This removed any incentive for retaining the land as far as the landlords were concerned and in 1878 The Epping Forest Act was passed establishing the entire area as a prototype "national park" and placing it in the care of the City of London. This far-sighted piece of legislation recognised the need to maintain the area as a place of recreation. It also stipulated that the 'natural aspect' of the forest should be maintained and the flora and fauna preserved. But ironically it stopped the right to cut wood which was one of the major factors which had triggered off the chain of events that led up to the 1878 Act. It is therefore safe to say that none of these pollarded trees have been cut since that date. So what has happened to the "natural aspect" of the forest since then?

'Well if you look at some of these trees you can see we have a problem. In a normal tree the trunk goes right up and divides with branches coming off at various heights but here, if you take this Beech, because of the way they have been cut, all the strain of the branches on the main trunk are imposed at one point. We know that traditionally the trees used to cut on a thirteen to fifteen year cycle but when you have a hundred years of growth you have these huge limbs and a terrific strain at one point on the tree. Furthermore, you tend to get rot in the centre of this crown as the rainwater lies in the hollow. So recently the trees have been losing their branches, especially since the drought of 1976, when a lot of them suffered

have Anglo-Saxon origins – East Ham, West Ham, Loughton and Waltham, for example. These settlers cleared large areas of the forest for firewood and timber, using the forest floor for grazing their livestock. Small-leaved Lime was used as fodder for cattle and for this they used to cut the young branches off in winter. This heavy cutting appears to have eventually eliminated the tree.

'About this time they started to pollard the trees. This form of management continued right through until the middle of the Nineteenth Century. Pollarding is not unlike coppicing in principle, except that the tree is cut about two metres (six to eight feet) above the ground so that the new shoots are out of reach of browsing animals such as deer and cattle. This pollarding had the effect of opening up the woodland severe stress. Also as the Beech grows so much faster than the oak, now that there is no pollarding, it is tending to shade-out some of the oaks and the overall species composition is becoming even more in favour of Beech. So one can say that the decision to let Epping Forest develop unchecked and to stop the pollarding is not wholly successful. If you leave a forest like

pecker with its laughing call is more a bird of the open areas, where it likes to feast on the ants' nests. The birch areas are especially favoured by warblers and Tree Pipits in the summer. But there is one bird of the Forest that I ought to mention and that is the Hawfinch. Epping has a special claim on this secretive bird as it was first proven as a British breeding species here in 1830 by

this for a hundred years, unfortunately you do not get natural forest, you simply get neglected man-managed woodland.'

The Beech trees for all this still looked magnificent with the orange leaves catching the autumn sun. As we made our way between them Paul pointed out the birdsong.

'A Robin is singing up there. They are in full song now as they set up their territories for the winter. Indeed, you almost get the impression that there is nothing but Robins in the Forest at times. Epping is very good for woodland birds all through the year. At the moment there will be flocks of Redpolls feeding on the birches. And in spring the woods are full of the high-pitched calls of tits and Nuthatches. The woodpeckers, in particular the Great Spotted, are often seen by visitors. We also have some Lesser Spotted Woodpeckers but the Green Wood-

Henry Doubleday. It is especially attracted by the Hornbeam which is an important component of sections of the wood. The Hawfinch has a very powerful beak which it uses to crack open even the strongest of nuts and fruits. It is very elusive but quite unmistakeable when you do see one, with its oversized beak and short-tail, rather like a top-heavy Chaffinch!'

We had now arrived at a gnarled old oak tree which was standing in a glade. It was pollarded like most of the other trees but its wide girth indicated that it was of great antiquity. Paul stood on one of the great bosses that covered the bole and peered inside the hollow trunk.

'It is amazing what you can find in these hollow trees – they are a haven for spiders and sheltering insects. Some contain bee hives and occasionally the more inaccessible

A pollarded tree that has keeled over littering the forest floor with its shed branches. If these are left they will provide an important habitat for a whole range of decomposing plants and insects.

An old pollarded oak which was also an important boundary tree. It is probably over 450 years old and, although completely hollow, is still producing a fine show of leaves.

Opposite **Standing like some fairy-tale tree in the autumn mist, this gnarled old Hornbeam clearly displays the marks of many years of pollarding. The wood of these fine old trees is so hard that it was used to make the teeth in the cog wheels of mills. A Holly is growing beside it.**

'In the south west of the country these old trees would be covered in lichens. But as Epping Forest lies on the north east side of London and gets the full brunt of the city's pollution, it has had a very impoverished lichen flora. We have early records of the lichens in the area and know that the number of species dropped from 120 to about 40. However, they are picking up again, whether this is a result of the Clean Air Acts of 1956 or conservation methods we are not sure.'

We now moved on deeper into the Forest. The shafts of autumn sunlight picked out the fallen leaves and bright green mosses. One of the most striking features was the amount of dead wood that covered the forest floor. Paul pointed out that these were left as a deliberate policy and that the decaying wood provided one of the most important ecological aspects of the Forest. We came to an old trunk of about four metres (fourteen feet) in height. It was the dead remains of an old pollarded oak; the branches had been cut back, as they would have been dangerous, but the trunk had been left standing. This made a superb micro-habitat for boring-beetles, spiders and fungi.

Further on we came to an area dominated by a new tree to our walk – the Hornbeam. These were pollarded like the Beeches but were very different in size. Paul told us about them.

'The Hornbeam pollards are the same age as the other trees, but are much smaller reflecting their much slower growth rate. Hornbeam tends to grow on the lower slopes as it needs a soil with a higher nutrient status than is found on the leached soils of the ridge. It is a tree which is sometimes confused with the Beech but once you know it, it is unmistakeable. The bark has a distinctive pattern, unlike the Beech, and its leaves are pointed with a double-toothed margin. The fruiting spike is also quite distinctive. Its name comes from the fact that its wood is very hard and is Saxon for "horny wooded tree". It was used for making yolks for oxen and wooden mallets. More interestingly it was used for the working parts of early machinery, for example, cog wheels in water and windmills. I have seen a huge cast iron mill wheel at Stratford-on-Bow in London where the teeth were made of Hornbeam. This was so that if the machinery jammed the teeth would act as a kind of "fuse" so the expensive iron wheel would be saved, but the wood was still hard enough to take everyday wear. It was also

ones even have bats roosting in them.

'This particular tree is interesting because it is a boundary pollard. We are actually standing on a manorial boundary which runs along the crest of the ridge. In the old days when they needed clear markers for surveying, certain old trees were deliberately left. This tree is just such a one and is probably about 450 years old. Pollarding tends to extend the life of some of these trees and you can see that, although it is completely hollow, it has a reasonable crown.

'These old pollards used to be rich in the epiphytic fern, Polypody, which would grow at the base of the crowns. However, the "Victorian Fern Craze" completely eradicated this fern from the area – an example of a species that has been destroyed not by habitat destruction but entirely by collecting by man.

The furiting spike and leaves of the Hornbeam on the forest floor, clearly showing the nuts which are sought after by squirrels and finches, including the elusive Hawfinch.

used for butchers' chopping blocks. Even today Hornbeam blunts the chain-saw blades faster than any of the other woods.

'The ground here is covered with the fruiting spikes of Hornbeam. This unfortunately is the result of Grey Squirrels stripping the trees; they cause an immense amount of damage and seem to definitely concentrate on Hornbeams around here. It is a tree that is also associated with certain birds. We have mentioned the Hawfinch, and little flocks of Greenfinches can be found feeding on them from August onwards.'

We had noticed many toadstools and bracket fungi on the forest floor, the older trees and fallen branches, providing bright splashes of colour amongst the autumn golds. Epping is justly famous for its woodland fungi, over a thousand species have been identified in the Forest. Every autumn it is a place of pilgrimage for many hundreds of people who come to see and pick the fruiting bodies of these strange members of the plant kingdom.

The following is a short guide to some of our more common and distinctive woodland fungi.

Bulgaria inquinans **Batchelor's or Pope's Buttons**. Fruit-bodies up to 3–4 centimetres across, with a gelantinous-rubbery consistency, often clustered together, like thick buttons with strongly convex lower surfaces; margins curved inwards at first, shining black and smooth on top, dark brown and scurfy below. Occurs on dead logs and branches of oak, less frequently beech or other trees. October to November: common.

Xylaria polymorpha **Dead-men's Fingers**. Fruit body club-shaped, sometimes grooved or with irregularities, 3–8 centimetres high, 1·5–2·5 centimetres wide, surface minutely pimpled, black; with a short black, cylindrical stem; flesh white with a black crust. Occurs singly or in clusters at the bases of dead stumps of broad-leaved trees, especially beech; throughout the year; common.

Fistulina hepatica **Beefsteak Fungus.** Fruitbody a rounded semicircular to tongue-shaped, 2–3 centimetres thick bracket, 10–25 centimetres across, sometimes with a short stalk-like base, blood-red to liver-coloured; the upper surface rough. Pores round, pale flesh coloured, the tubes separate from each other if the surface is flexed. Flesh red, rather fibrous, yielding a reddish juice; the surface layer gelatinous. Spore deposit pinkish brown. Occurs on trunks of living oaks or occasionally other trees, causing the wood to turn rich brown before decaying; the so-called 'Brown Oak' disease. August to November, fairly common. Best

Bachelor's Buttons
(*Bulgaria inquinans*).

Dead-men's Fingers
(*Xylaria polymorpha*).

cooked as cubes added to stews when it has a pleasant acid flavour.

Piptoporus (Polyporus, Ungulina) betulinus
Razor-strop Fungus or **Birch Polypore**
Cap thick, soft and bun-like, semicircular to kidney- or hoof-shaped, sometimes almost circular, stemless and broadly to narrowly attached, 8–15 centimetres across, 2–5 centimetres thick with a thick rounded margin. Upper surface shallowly convex and smooth, with a thin greyish or very pale brownish, separable skin. Tubes up to 10 millimetres long; pores small 0·15–0·25 millimetres across, round and white. Flesh white, softly corky. Occurs on living and dead birch trunks, causing their death; summer and autumn, very common, dried specimens found at all times. The flesh was formerly cut into strips, mounted on wood and used for stropping razors. It has also been used by entomologists for mounting small insects.

Pleurotus ostreatus **Oyster Mushroom** Cap 7–13 centimetres across, shell-shaped to rounded flap-shape, convex, later flattening; deep bluish grey in colour to almost black when young, becoming smoky brown or pale yellowish to umber. Usually many clustered together, with a narrow point of attachment or with a short thick, white stem, 2–3 centimetres × 1–2 centimetres attached

Top **Beefsteak Fungus** (*Fistulina hepatica*).

Above **Razor-strop Fungus or Birch Polypore** (*Piptoporus betulinus*).

towards or at one side with a woolly base. Gills white, becoming pale yellowish, deeply decurrent and anastomosing at the base. Flesh white and a little fibrous. Spore deposit lilac in the mass. Occurs on trunks, stumps etc., usually of broad leaved trees, especially beech; throughout the year; common.

Boletus edulis **Ceps or Cèpe** Cap 6–20 centimetres across, date-brown to bay, chestnut or dark brick, more or less flattened convex; margin whitish or with a white line; surface smooth to slightly rough, slightly sticky in wet weather. Tubes white, becoming greyish yellow, with small round, similarly coloured pores. Stem 3–23 centi-

metres × 3–7 centimetres, often rather robust, cylindrical to club-shaped or bulbous, light tawny or buff to whitish with a raised white network of veins usually confined to the upper half. Flesh white not turning blue. Occurs under broad-leaved or coniferous trees. August to November; common. A well-known and popular edible species, often used for making dried 'mushroom' soups. *B. aestivalis* (*reticulatus*) is very similar but usually has a paler coloured cap, often cinnamon to pale snuff-brown, without a whitish margin, network on the stem usually extends onto the base. Common under beech and oak. *B. pinicola* is also very similar but has a dark purplish brown cap and a wine-coloured stem with pale blood

red tints on the network and the flesh tinged wine-red; occurs under pines.

Amongst numerous other species of *Boletus*, *B. piperatus* deserves a mention since it is unique in having a peppery taste. The cap is 3–8 centimetres across and cinnamon-brown; stem the same colour, slender 4–7 centimetres × 0·5–2 centimetres, bright yellow at the base. The pores are rust-brown, large and angular. Occurs in woods and on heaths in autumn; frequent. *B. satanas*, the Devil's Boletus, is the only poisonous species and is recognized by the whitish cap, blood red pores and stem with a red network of veins at the apex. It is uncommon and occurs under broad-leaved trees on limy soils.

Above **Oyster Mushroom** (*Pleurotus ostreatus*).

Below **Ceps** (*Boletus edulis*).

Russula ochroleuca **Common Yellow Russula** (or Brittle-gill) Cap 4–12 centimetres across, ochre, yellow or sometimes yellowish green, margin smooth, later furrowed. Gills creamy. Stem 4–7 centimetres × 1·5–2·5 centimetres, somewhat fragile, white, greying with age, especially when water-logged. Taste from mild to moderately hot. Spores whitish to cream. Occurs under broadleaved and coniferous trees. August to November, mainly October; very common, the commonest of the russulas and one of the commonest of all agarics.

Amanita muscaria **Fly Agaric** Cap 10–20 centimetres across, scarlet or orange, sometimes fading to yellow, rounded at first, later expanding to convex, finally flattening, covered at first with white, flattish to thick warts, usually abundant but at times disappearing, slimy when moist, margin slightly striate. Gills white, free and closely spaced. Stem 10–22 centimetres × 2·5 centimetres, white, solid but later hollow, striate above the white, skirt-like ring situated near the top, base bulbous, with concentric rings of white, woolly scales. Occurs under birches and pines; August to November; fairly common. The name comes from its use as a fly poison. Also called the 'Sacred Mushroom' as it was used to produce hallucinations in religious practices. However, it is dangerously poisonous.

Oudemansiella (Armillaria, Mucidula) mucida **Slimy Beech Cap** Cap 3–8 centimetres across, white, slightly greyish or tinged brownish, convex, later flattening, very slimy or glutinous, rather translucent; margin sometimes striate. Gills white, broad adnate or adnexed with a decurrent tooth and well-spaced. Stem 4–7·5 centimetres × 4–15 millimetres, white, striate above the white, horizontal or drooping, membranous ring on its upper half, somewhat scaly below it, rather tough and fibrous. Occurs on living or dead beech trunks or branches, often high up a tree and often many together; August to November; common.

Laccaria laccata **The Deceiver** Cap 3–5 centimetres across, reddish brown or tawny to brick-red when moist, paling to ochre-yellow or dull yellowish when dry, hygrophanous, with a sharp distinction between moist and dry regions, convex, later flattening, sometimes umbilicate; surface often breaking up into small scurfy scales; margin often waved and crisped, striate when moist. Gills mauvy pinkish, white-powdered when mature, adnate with a decurrent tooth, broad and well spaced. Stem 5–10 centimetres × 6–10 millimetres, the same colour as the cap or darker, often longitudinally streaked, fibrous, toughish, curved and twisted, base white and woolly. Occurs in woods and on heaths; July to December; one of the commonest of agarics. Very variable in appearance and often difficult to recognize at first sight, hence the common name, but a glance at the gills, which have a peculiar colour shade and pattern that once known is easily remembered, is usually sufficient to identify it. *L. proxima* is very

similar but tends to be larger and taller and grows in damper places. Its spores are oval instead of spherical as in the last species.

Hypholoma (Naematoloma) fasciculare **Sulphur Tuft** Cap 2–5 centimetres across, pale yellow, often reddish brown in the centre, convex, later flattening, sometimes with a raised area in the centre, smooth; margin incurved, often with brownish, thin, skinny fragments of the veil. Gills greenish yellow at first, later becoming dull olive-green or chocolate, sinuate and closely spaced. Stem 5–22 centimetres × 4–10 millimetres, pale yellow, cylindrical, often wavy or curved, fibrillose, becoming hollow, often with a band of fibres from the veil near the top. Taste bitter. Flesh yellow, fibrous in the stem; turns orange with ammonia at the base of the stem. Occurs in clusters that are often very large, on and around stumps of broad-leaved trees, all the year round though mainly in autumn; the commonest of the agarics. Poisonous.

Scleroderma citrinum (S. aurantium, S. vulgare) **Common Earth-ball**. Fruit-body 4–8 centimetres across, globose to pumpkin-shaped, sometimes shallowly lobed; surface firm, whitish or dull yellow-ish, cracking into small, flat, more or less brownish warts. The base is blunt and attached to mycelial cords. The flesh of the outer layer is 3–6 millimetres thick, white and often becomes pinkish when cut. It surrounds an inner, hard mass, which is greyish, at first, then purplish black and with whitish veins, and finally dull brown and powdery. The fruit-body eventually splits open irregularly or decays away. Occurs on the ground in woods, on heaths, etc.; July to January; very common. Although reported as sometimes being used as a substitute for truffles, it is also said to have been the cause of serious poisoning, *S. verrucosum* is similar and occurs in the same places, though less commonly, but is often larger, is thinner walled and is attached at the base by a mass of root-like cords. The spore mass is finally olive-brown.

Phallus impudicus **Stinkhorn or Wood Witch**. Fruit-body, when young, white or yellowish, egg-like to globose, 3–5 centi-metres across, with a thin skin covering a thick jelly layer which surrounds the compressed stem and spore mass. It is attached by a thick, white mycelial cord. At maturity the stem expands and breaks out of the egg and is topped by a thimble-like cap. Stem 10–30 centimetres × 1–3 centimetres, white cylindrical, narrowing at both ends, spongy (like expanded polystyrene) and hollow. Cap 3–5 centimetres high, attached only to the apex of the stem, covered with a slimy, blackish olive, foetid spore mass. This is removed eventually by flies feeding on it to reveal the white, honeycomb-like surface of the cap which has at its apex a small, white disc with a central hole. The foetid odour may be detected when several metres away. Occurs on the ground in woods and in gardens; May to November; common.

Above **Common Earth-ball** (*Scleroderma citrinum*).

Above left **Stinkhorn** (*Phallus impudicus*).

Descriptions of Mushrooms from *Hamlyn Nature Guides: Mushrooms and Toadstools* by Ronald Rayner.

Above **Fly Agaric**
(*Amanita muscaria*).

Left **Slimy Beech Cap**
(*Oudemansiella mucida*).

Right **The Deceiver**
(*Laccaria laccata*).

Further reading

Bang, P. and Dahlstrom, P., *Animal Tracks and Signs*, Collins (1974).

Bellamy, D. J., *Bellamy on Botany*, BBC Publications (1972, revised 1975).

Bellamy, D. J., *Bellamy's Britain*, BBC Publications (1974).

Bellamy, D. J., *Botanic Man*, Hamlyn (1978).

Brown, R. W. and Lawrence M. J., *Mammals of Britain*, Blandford (1967, revised 1974).

Bruun, B. and Singer, A., *The Hamlyn Guide to Birds of Britain and Europe*, Hamlyn (1970, revised 1978).

Chinery, M., *A Field Guide to the Insects of Britain and Northern Europe*, Collins (1973).

Corbet, G. B. and Southern, H. N. (eds.), *The Handbook of British Mammals*, Blackwell (1977).

Darlington, A., *The Pocket Encyclopaedia of Plant Galls*, Blandford (1968, revised 1975).

Holliday, F. G. T., *Wildlife of Scotland*, Macmillan (1979).

Hubbard, C. E., *Grasses*, Penguin (1968).

Humphries, C. J., Press, J. R., Sutton, D. A., *The Hamlyn Guide to Trees of Britain and Europe*, Hamlyn (1981).

Mabey, R., *The Common Ground*, Arrow (1981).

Measures, D., *Bright Wings of Summer*, Cassell (1977).

Morris, P. (ed.), *The Natural History of the British Isles*, Country Life (1979).

Phillips, R., *Grasses, Ferns, Mosses and Lichens of Great Britain and Ireland*, Pan (1980).

Pollard, E., Hooper, M. D. and Moore, N. W., *Hedges*, Collins (1974).

Rackham, O., *Trees and Woodland in the British Landscape*, Dent (1976).

Rayner, R., *Hamlyn Nature Guides: Mushrooms and Toadstools*, Hamlyn (1979).

Rose, F., *Wildflower Key*, Warne (1981).

Simms, E., *Woodland Birds*, Collins (1971).

Wilkinson, G., *Epitaph for the Elm*, Hutchinson (1978).

Whalley, P., *Butterfly Watching*, Severn House (1980).

Organisations to join

Botanical Society of the British Isles
68 Outwoods Road, Loughborough, Leicestershire.
A national society for both amateur and professional botanists. Organises mapping schemes and is active in the conservation of our wild plants.

British Butterfly Conservation Society
Tudor House, Quorn, Leicester.

British Trust for Conservation Volunteers
10–14 Duke Street, Reading, Berkshire RG1 4RU.
An organisation for people over sixteen years of age which undertakes practical projects, such as clearing scrub, maintaining reserves, tree-planting, etc.

British Trust for Ornithology
Beech Grove, Tring, Hertfordshire.
National organisation which carries out research into all aspects of bird life supported by a growing army of amateur enthusiasts.

Ramblers' Association
1–5 Wandsworth Road, London SW8 2LJ.

Royal Society for Nature Conservation
The Green, Nettleham, Lincoln.
The Royal Society for Nature Conservation is the national association of the 42 local Nature Conservation Trusts which form the major voluntary organisation concerned with all aspects of wildlife conservation in the United Kingdom. The Trusts have a combined membership of 140,000 and, together with the Society, own or manage over 1,300 nature reserves throughout the UK covering a range of sites, from woodland and heathland to wetland and estuarine habitats. Most Trusts have full-time staff but the members themselves, with a wide range of skills, contribute greatly to all aspects of the work.

Royal Society for the Protection of Birds
The Lodge, Sandy, Bedfordshire.
The major conservation organisation for birds and their habitats.

The Scottish Wildlife Trust
25 Johnston Terrace, Edinburgh EH1 2NH.
The Scottish branch of the County Conservation Trusts.

Watch: The Watch Trust for Environmental Education
22 The Green, Nettleham, Lincoln LN2 2NR.
Sponsored by *The Sunday Times* and the *Royal Society for Nature Conservation;* WATCH is a national club for children and young teenagers.

The Woodland Trust
37 Westgate, Grantham, Lincolnshire NG31 6LL.
Charity dedicated to protecting our woodland heritage; has a growing number of reserves.

World Wildlife Fund
29 Greville Street, London EC1N 8AX.

Index

Figures in italics refer to illustrations

Places of interest

see Information pages
for further details

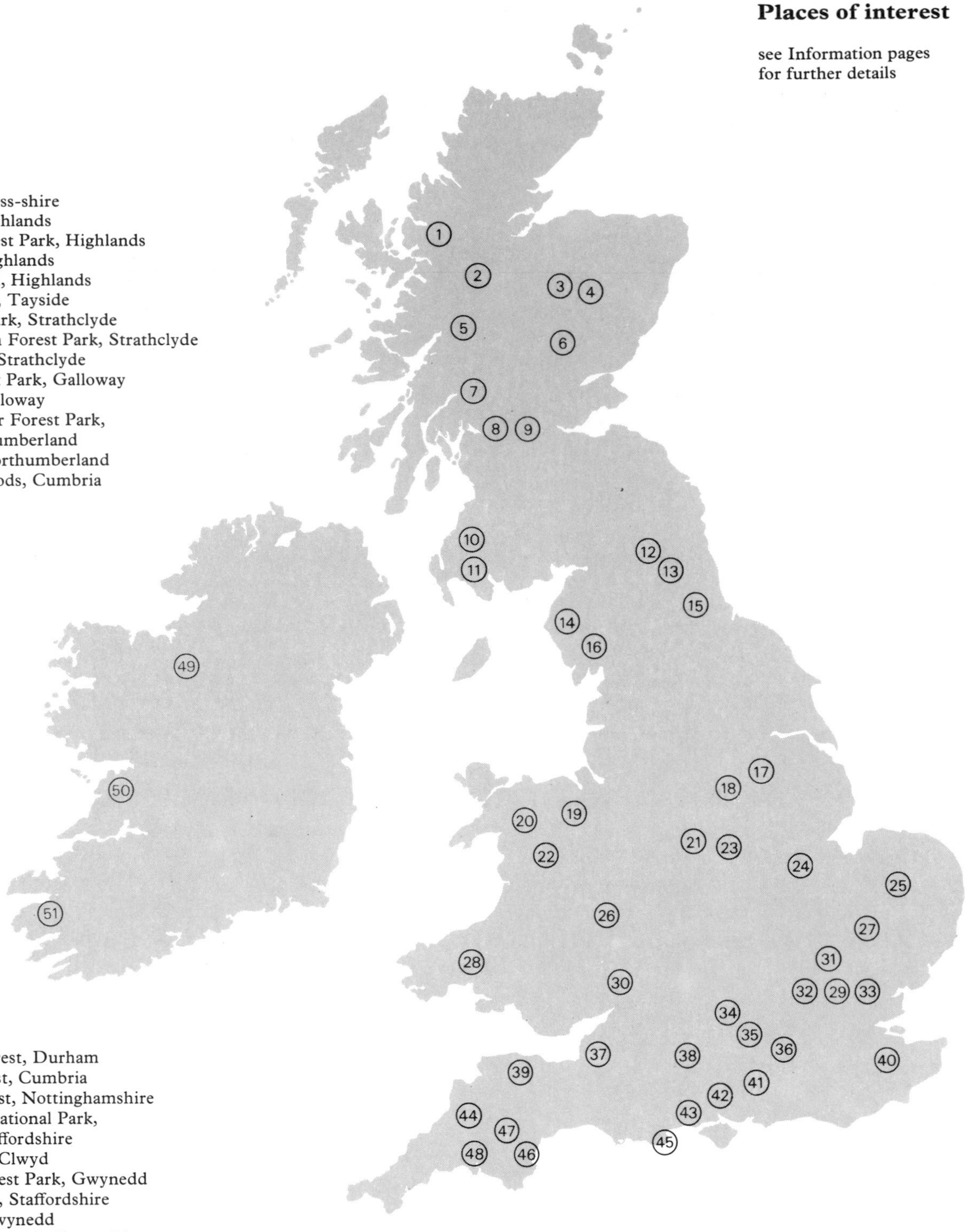

1 Beinn Eighe, Ross-shire
2 Glen Affric, Highlands
3 Glen More Forest Park, Highlands
4 Cairngorms, Highlands
5 Arriundle Wood, Highlands
6 Rannoch Forest, Tayside
7 Argyll Forest Park, Strathclyde
8 Queen Elizabeth Forest Park, Strathclyde
9 Loch Lomond, Strathclyde
10 Galloway Forest Park, Galloway
11 Glen Trool, Galloway
12 Border's/Kielder Forest Park,
   Borders/ Northumberland
13 Allen Banks, Northumberland
14 Borrowdale Woods, Cumbria

15 Hamsterley Forest, Durham
16 Grizedale Forest, Cumbria
17 Sherwood Forest, Nottinghamshire
18 Peak District National Park,
   Derbyshire/Staffordshire
19 Clwyd Forest, Clwyd
20 Snowdonia Forest Park, Gwynedd
21 Cannock Chase, Staffordshire
22 Maentwrog, Gwynedd
23 Charnwood Forest, Leicestershire
24 Woodwalton Fen, Cambridgeshire
25 Thetford Chase, Norfolk
26 Wyre Forest, Herefordshire/Worcestershire
27 Bradfield Woods, Suffolk
28 Dinas Woodlands, Dyfed
29 Hainault Forest, Essex
30 Forest of Dean, Herefordshire
31 Hatfield Forest, Essex
32 Epping Forest, Essex
33 Norsey Wood, Essex
34 Burnham Beeches, Buckinghamshire
35 Windsor Forest, Berkshire
36 Box Hill, Surrey
37 Ebbor Gorge, Somerset
38 Saversnake, Wiltshire

39 Lynmouth, Devon
40 Scords Wood, Kent
41 Selborne, Hampshire
42 Kingley Vale, Hampshire
43 New Forest, Hampshire/Dorset
44 Lydford Gorge, Devon
45 Brownsea Island, Dorset
46 Yarner Wood, Devon
47 Wistman's Wood, Devon
48 Goodameavy, Devon
49 Correl Glen Forest, Fermanagh
50 Burren, Clare
51 Killarney Oakwoods, Kerry

The Hamlyn Leisure Atlas Series

Each book 128 pages. Illustrated with colour and black-and-white artwork and photographs.
30.3 x 21.6cm

These are the most comprehensive guides to regions of Britain, each with many hundreds of places to visit and things to do, clearly marked on superb six-colour maps at the easy-to-read scale of 1.6 miles to 1 inch and described in a detailed gazetteer section. The maps are the most detailed available in any atlas at this scale, showing trunk roads, country lanes, natural and man-made features and a wealth of geographical detail, with a unique colour-coded height presentation providing a graphic picture of the countryside. These specially prepared maps comprise unrivalled atlasses of their regions. Each atlas features an introductory section which includes an illustrated regional profile, with chapters on food and drink, history and legend, flora and fauna and much more; there is also a calendar of events and a comprehensive index to the maps.

Hamlyn Leisure Atlas –
North Country
0 600 34997 7

Hamlyn Leisure Atlas –
Southern England
0 600 34998 5

Hamlyn Leisure Atlas –
Wales
0 600 34956 X

Hamlyn Leisure Atlas –
West Country
0 600 34957 8

Discovering the Countryside with
David Bellamy

This exciting series of books introduces the reader to a new way of looking at the countryside. Each book has been designed for the many people who delight in spending their weekends and holidays exploring rural Britain. All too often, the interested walker can name the separate elements that make up the landscape but is unable to take this knowledge further. *Discovering the Countryside* shows how to begin to understand the intricate world of our animals and plants. Each book is based around an overall habitat and contains walks with naturalists from throughout Britain. Every walk looks at a different aspect of the environment, giving us a privileged glimpse of the countryside as seen through the eyes of experts. They are illustrated with superb especially commissioned colour and black and white photographs.

Professor David Bellamy, as consultant editor and contributor, has added his own inimitable touch to the series and has ensured that each book is an enjoyable as well as stimulating journey around our countryside. Together with David Bellamy, the Royal Society for Nature Conservation has collaborated in the production of the series.

Also available
Discovering the Countryside with David Bellamy
Coastal Walks
0 600 35588 8

This companion volume explores our varied coastline with chapters on a wide range of habitats from shingle beaches and sand dunes to rocky shores and estuaries.

Books in preparation
Discovering the Countryside with David Bellamy
Waterside Walks
0 600 35636 1

Discovering the Countryside with David Bellamy
Grassland Walks
0 600 35637 X